MEATLESS MEALS For WORKING PEOPLE

Quick and Easy Vegetarian Recipes

By Debra Wasserman
& Charles Stahler

Baltimore, Maryland

Second Edition, 1998

The recipes in this book were tested and developed on the Appalachian Trail, the Delaware shore, at food demonstrations in Maryland, in hotel rooms in Rhode Island, and several other places, which necessitated quick and easy dishes.

Debra Wasserman and Charles Stahler are Co-directors of The Vegetarian Resource Group and founding editors of *Vegetarian Journal*.

Acknowledgements

Special thanks to Reed Mangels, Ph.D., R.D., for doing the nutritional analysis for all the recipes and contributing her expertise to this book. Thank you also to the following individuals who provided information: Jeanne Bartas, Ruth Blackburn, M.S., R.D., Suzanne Havala, M.S., R.D., Marie Henein, Barbara Lovitts, Ph.D., Stephanie Reph, Brad Scott, Annabelle Simpson, Marna Golub-Smith, Ellen Tattenbaum, Linda Tyler, and Mike Vogel. And finally, thank you to Israel and Eva Mossman for proof-reading the entire manuscript and John Peters for doing all the wonderful illustrations.

Please note: The contents of *Meatless Meals for Working People* are not intended to provide medical advice. Medical advice should be obtained from a qualified health professional.

Library of Congress Cataloging-in-Publication Data
Meatless Meals for Working People — Quick and Easy
Vegetarian Recipes (Second Edition)/
Debra Wasserman and Charles Stahler
Library of Congress Catalog Card Number: 98-60485

ISBN 0-931411-19-X

10 9 8 7 6 5 4 3 2

Table of Contents

Salads and Dressings

Soups

Lunch Ideas

Side Dishes

Side Dishes (continued)

Main Dishes

Soy Dishes

Chinese Cuisine

Mexican Fiesta

Spreads and Dips

Desserts

Vegetarianism in a Nutshell

Vegetarianism is the abstinence from meat, fish, or fowl. Among the many reasons for being a vegetarian are compassion for animals, aesthetic considerations, and ecological, economic, spiritual, and health reasons. The American Dietetic Association has affirmed that a vegetarian diet can meet all known nutrient needs. Like every diet, the key to a healthy vegetarian diet is simple. Eat a variety of foods, eat a lot of greens, and have high-fat, high-salt, empty-calorie foods as only a small part of your diet. For the growing number of vegetarians who are following a vegan life-style and abstain from all animal products, including milk, cheese, eggs, and honey, this also can be done easily, but you may want to talk to others who have been practicing this diet.

Fresh is Best, But...

Using frozen, canned, and prepackaged foods greatly decreases food preparation time whether you are on a vegetarian diet or a non-vegetarian diet. Beware, however, that many prepackaged foods are high in sodium and may have animal shortening in them.

FROZEN FOODS

Frozen foods can be stored easily, and quickly popped into the oven or microwave while you're changing your clothes after work. Frozen vegetables such as green beans, corn, and spinach can be cooked in a short time and eaten alone or combined with other ingredients. Be careful not to overcook the vegetables or use too much water when cooking them. Pillsbury offers several frozen pasta and vegetable mixes under the Green Giant label. Many supermarkets carry frozen vegetarian entrées manufactured by natural foods companies, which can be served for lunch or dinner.

CANNED AND PREPACKAGED VEGETARIAN FOODS

Though often more expensive than preparing from scratch, there are numerous canned and prepackaged foods you can find in most supermarkets. These items can quickly be used to prepare a meal or simply have a snack.

DAIRY CASE

Your dairy case is packed full of vegetarian ingredients and fast meal possibilities. Corn and wheat tortillas can easily be heated up and stuffed with leftover bean, grain, and/or vegetable mixtures.

Suggested Vegetarian Meals

Listed below are quick dishes and food items that you probably know how to cook already and can be made from common foods found in supermarkets. For a main meal, you may have one large central dish, a sandwich with or without soup, or several side dishes. Remember, the key to any healthy diet is variety.

BREAKFAST ITEMS:

These can easily be served as part of a main meal. Try to limit your use of eggs. You can substitute 1 small mashed banana for each egg when making the batter for French Toast or using pancake and waffle mixes.

Frozen Breakfast Foods
Bagels
Biscuits
French Toast
Meatless Breakfast Patties and Links
Pancakes
Waffles

Other Breakfast Foods
Breads (English muffins, cornbread, rye, etc.)
Dry Cereal (Grape-Nuts, Muesli, Nutri-Grain, etc.)
Hot Cereal (Cream of Rice and Cream of Wheat, Farina, Grits,
    Oatmeal, Wheatena, etc.)
Fresh Fruits
Fruit Butters (apple butter, etc.)
Granola
Health Valley Cereal Bars
Jams (Fruit sweetened variety is best)
Wheat Germ
Yogurt

SANDWICHES:

Nut butter (peanut, cashew, almond) and jam
Bagels and hummus (chickpea spread)
Nut butter and sliced fruit (banana, apple, pear)
Hunts Manwich Sloppy Joe Sauce and vegetables
Baked beans and lettuce on toast
Tofu salad (mashed tofu, minced celery, grated
    carrot, sweet relish, mayonnaise)
Chickpea salad (mashed chickpeas, grated carrot,
    minced celery, dill weed, mayonnaise)

Breads
Bagels
English Muffins
French bread
Garlic bread (often found in freezer case)
Hard rolls
Italian bread
Kaiser rolls
Pita bread
Raisin bread
Rye bread
Tortillas
Whole wheat bread

MAIN MEALS (lunch or dinner):
Frozen Main Dishes
The following list is by no means complete, rather just a start.

Garden Burger (Wholesome and Hearty)
        Original
        Vegan
        Vegetable Medley

Harvest Burger (Worthington Foods, Inc.)
        Italian Style
        Original Flavor
        Protein Crumbles

Healthy Choice
    Pasta Shells Marinara
    Zucchini Lasagna
    (Caution: Garden Potato Casserole contains
        chicken broth)

Morningstar Farm's
    Better'n Burger
    Chik Nuggets
    Chik Patties
    Garden Vegetable Patties
    Meatless Grillers
    Spicy Black Bean Burgers

Old El Paso
    Bean and Cheese Burrito

Patio
    Burrito-Bean and Cheese

Royal Duchess
    Frozen Falafel

Stouffer's
    Cheese Enchiladas
    Cheese Shells
    Fettucine Alfredo
    Potatoes Au Gratin
    Scalloped Potatoes
    Vegetable Lasagna
    (Caution: Stouffer's Noodles Romanoff
        contains gelatin)

Stouffer's Lean Cuisine
    Marinara Twist
    Three Bean Chili
    Zucchini Lasagna

Stouffer's Lean Cuisine—Lunch Express
        Alfredo Pasta Primavera
        Penne Pasta with Tomato Basil Sauce

Weight Watcher's Smart Ones
        Angel Hair Pasta
        Lasagna Florentine
        Ravioli Florentine

Woodstock Whole Earth Foods, Inc.
        The Better Burger

Don't forget that many types of vegetarian frozen pizza are
available, too.

ETHNIC FOODS FOR MAIN MEALS (LUNCH OR DINNER):

Asian
Canned Vegetables (Water Chestnuts, Baby Corn, etc.)
Fortune Cookies
Mustards
Rice Noodles
Sauces (be sure to watch out for non-vegetarian fats
    and broths)

Jewish
Borscht
Falafel Mix
Hummus
Kasha
Mandlen (soup nuts)
Matzo
Matzo Ball Mix
Matzo Meal
Potato Pancakes
Soup Mixes
Tahini (sesame butter)
Tam Tam Crackers

Mexican
Burrito and Taco Kits
Fajita Marinade
Salsa
Taco Sauces
Taco Seasoning Mixes
Tortillas and Taco Shells
Vegetarian Refried Beans (without lard)

Middle Eastern
Falafel Mix
Hummus (canned)
Hummus Mix
Tahini Sauce

PASTA
Most pasta sold in packages in supermarkets do not contain eggs, unless it is called egg pasta. Fresh pasta often does contain eggs. Look for brands such as Mueller's and San Giorgio.

PASTA SAUCES:
Contadina
> Garden Vegetable
> Marinara
> Mushroom and Green Bell Pepper
> Tomato, Garlic, and Onion

Classico
> Mushrooms and Ripe Olives
> Spicy Red Pepper
> Tomato and Basil

Newman's Own
> All Natural Marinara Style Venetian Spaghetti Sauce
> Bombolina
> Sockarooni Spaghetti Sauce

Prego
    Diced Onion and Garlic
    Garden Combination
    Traditional
    Zesty Basil
    Zesty Oregano with Mushroom

Ragu Chunky Gardenstyle
    Chunky Garden Combination
    Chunky Mushroom & Green Pepper
    Chunky Tomato, Garlic, Onion
    Super Vegetable Primavera

Ragu Fino Italiano
    Garlic and Basil
    Tomato and Herb

Ragu Light
    Garden Harvest
    No Sugar Added
    Tomato & Herb

Ragu Old World Style
    Mushroom
    Traditional

Ragu Thick and Hearty
    Mushroom
    Tomato & Herb

VEGETARIAN DRY MIXES TO MAKE MAIN MEALS:

Fantastic Foods
    Falafil
    Hummus
    Nature's Burger
    Refried Beans
    Tabouli
    Vegetarian Chili

DAIRY CASE ITEMS:
Biscuits
Cookie Dough
Dips
Flour and Corn Tortillas
Fruit Salad in Jars
Guacamole
Juice
Pie Crusts
Refrigerated Pastas
Rolls
Salsa
Yogurt

ITEMS FOUND IN PRODUCE SECTION BESIDES PRODUCE:
Chopped Garlic, Jalapeño Peppers, etc.
Croutons
Fruit Dips (Chocolate and Caramel)
Powdered Soup/Salad/Dip Mixes
Salad Dressings
Sun-Dried Tomatoes
Tofu
Toppings for Baked Potatoes/ Salads

ITEMS FOUND IN THE DELI COUNTER:
Cole Slaw
Dilled Cucumbers
Hummus
Macaroni Salad
Olives
Pasta Salad
Potato Salad
Tabouli
Vegetable Salads

SIDE DISHES:
B & M 99% Fat Free Vegetarian Baked Beans
Bush's Vegetarian Baked Beans
Campbell's Vegetarian Beans in Tomato Sauce
Furman's Vegetarian Beans and Sauce
Green Giant Barbecue Beans
Green Giant Mexican Beans
Health Valley Fat-Free Chili with Black Beans
Heinz Vegetarian Beans in Tomato Sauce
Old El Paso Vegetarian Refried Beans

<u>Canned Beans</u>
Black Beans
Black Eyed Peas
Cannellini (White Kidney Beans)
Fava Beans
Garbanzo Beans (Chickpeas)
Northern Beans
Pinto Beans
Red Kidney Beans

<u>Dried Beans</u> (Hint: Use a pressure cooker for quick
    and easy cooking of dried beans)
Baby Lima Beans
Black Beans
Black Eyed Peas
Garbanzo Beans (Chickpeas)
Great Northern Beans
Green Split Peas
Kidney Beans
Lentils
Lima Beans
Mixed Beans for Soups
Navy Beans
Northern Beans
Pinto Beans
Roman Beans
Yellow Split Peas

Frozen Side Dishes
Empire Kosher Potato Pancakes
French Fries
Gabila's Potato Knishes
Garlic Bread
Hashbrowns
Mashed Potatoes
Onion Rings
Stuffed Potatoes
Tater Tots
Twice Baked Potatoes
Vegetable and Pasta Combinations

Grains
Casbah
       Bulgur Pilaf
       Couscous
       Lentil Pilaf
       Rice Pilaf
       Spanish Pilaf
       Tabouli

Fantastic Foods
       Imported Couscous
       Imported Basmati Rice
       Tabouli Salad Mix

Good Shepherd
       Bulgur Wheat

Knorr
       Risotto-Onion Herb
       Risotto-Mushroom
       Risotto-Milanese
       Spicy Couscous-Raisin and Almond

Near East
    Couscous
    Taboule Wheat Salad Mix
    Wheat Pilaf

Old World
    Bulgur Wheat

Quaker
    Barley

Reese
    Wheat Pilaf Mix—Middle Eastern Style
    Taboule Wheat Salad Mix Middle East Style

Rice Select
    Jasmati Rice
    Texmati Rice

Uncle Ben's
    Brown Rice

Wolff's
    Kasha

Instant Seasoned Rice
Lipton Rice and Sauce
    Alfredo Broccoli
    Cajun Style
    Cheddar Broccoli
    Herb and Butter
    Mushroom
    Spanish

Mahatma One Step Dish
    Saffron Yellow Seasonings and Rice

Near East
> Long Grain and Wild Rice Pilaf
> Spanish Rice Pilaf

Rice A Roni
> Fried Rice with Almonds
> Long Grain and Wild Rice (Original)
> Spanish Rice

R.M. Quigg's
> Golden Paella Rice Mix
> Herb Rice
> Long Grain and Wild Rice
> Original Yellow Rice

Uncle Ben's
> Long Grain and Wild Rice-Original Recipe

Zatarain's
> Dirty Rice Mix

Canned Vegetables
Artichokes
Asparagus
Beets
Carrots
Collard Greens
Corn (Regular and Cream Style)
Green Beans
Green Peas
Hearts of Palm
Hominy
Kale
Lima Beans
Mixed Vegetables
Mushrooms

Okra
Sauerkraut
Spinach
Succotash (Lima Beans and Corn)
Sweet Peas
Sweet Potatoes
Tomatoes
Turnip Greens
Wax Beans
White Potatoes
Yams

Frozen Vegetables
Artichoke Hearts
Asparagus
Bell Peppers
Black Eye Peas
Broccoli
Brussels Sprouts
Carrots
Cauliflower
Collard Greens
Corn
Green Beans
Green Peas
Kale
Lima Beans
Mixed Vegetables
Mustard Greens
Okra
Onions
Peas and Carrots
Spinach
Squash
Succotash
Turnip Greens

SOUPS:
Baxters
>Vichyssoise
>Minestrone Soup
>Potato and Leek Soup--Vegetarian Recipe
>Bean and Mixed Pepper Soup

Bean Cuisine (Dry Seasoned Mixes found either near canned soups or dry beans)
>Thick as Fog Split Pea
>Santa Fe Corn Chowder
>Island Black Bean
>13 Bean Bouillabaisse
>Ultima Pasta E Fagioli
>White Bean Provencal

Campbell's
>Italian Tomato
>Black Bean
>Tomato
>Vegetarian Vegetable
>Tomato Bisque
>Old Fashioned Tomato Rice
>Hearty Vegetable with Pasta
>Golden Corn
>Green Pea (Not Split Pea!)
>Tomato Rice

Campbell's Chunky Soup
>Vegetable Soup
>Mediterranean Vegetable Soup

Campbell's Home Cookin'
>Lentil

Campbell's Soup and Recipe Mix (Powdered)
>Onion Soup

Da Vinci Soup
   Minestrone
   Macaroni & Bean-Pasta E Fagioli

Dominique's Original Recipe
   Gazpacho Soup

Fantastic Foods (Cups of Soup)
   Vegetable Tomato Ramen Noodles
   Curry Vegetable Instant Ramen Soup

Hain Naturals—99% Fat Free Soup
   Wild Rice
   Black Bean
   Vegetarian Lentil

Health Valley
   Organic Tomato Soup
   Organic Vegetable Soup
   Organic Black Bean Soup

Health Valley Fat-Free Soup
   14 Garden Vegetable
   5 Bean Vegetable
   Vegetable Barley
   Real Italian Minestrone
   Tomato Vegetable

Healthy Choice
   Country Vegetable
   Garden Vegetable
   Lentil

Knorr
   Vegetable Soup and Recipe Mix
   Leek Soup and Recipe Mix
   Tomato with Basil Soup and Recipe Mix

Fine Herb Soup and Recipe Mix
Spinach Soup and Recipe Mix
Black Bean Soup Cup
Vegetarian Vegetable Bouillon

Lipton Recipe Soup Mix Recipe Secrets (Powder)
Onion
Italian Herb with Tomato
Onion-Mushroom
Vegetable

Nile Spice (Cups)
Minestrone Soup
Black Bean Soup
Split Pea Soup
Red Beans & Rice
Lentil Soup

Progresso Healthy Classics
Lentil Soup
Minestrone Soup

Progresso Pasta Soups
Hearty Vegetable & Rotini
Hearty Minestrone
Lentil and Shells
Hearty Tomato & Pasta

Progresso Soup
Lentil
Tomato
Macaroni and Bean
Minestrone (Original Recipe; NOT Zesty Minestrone)

Townhouse (Safeway Store Brand)
Tomato Soup

Lipton Recipe Secrets Soup Mix (Boxed)
    Onion
    Onion and Mushroom
    Vegetable

GRAVY AND SAUCES:

Franco-American
    Mushroom Gravy

Hunt's
    Manwich Sloppy Joe Sauce

McCormick Powdered Sauces/Seasonings
    Chili Seasoning
    Hot Chili Seasoning
    Sloppy Joe Seasoning
    Spaghetti Sauce Mix Italian Style
    Spaghetti Sauce Mix—Thick and Zesty

McCormick Pasta Prima Powdered Sauces
    Alfredo Pasta Sauce Blend
    Herb and Garlic Pasta Sauce Blend

Crown Colony (Safeway Store Brand)
    Alfredo Pasta Sauce Mix
    Chili Seasoning
    Sloppy Joe Seasoning
    Spaghetti with Mushrooms Sauce Mix
    Spaghetti Sauce Mix
    Stroganoff Sauce Mix

SNACK ITEMS:
Cookies
Corn Chips
Dips
Dried Fruits (Raisins, Dates, Prunes, Figs, etc.)
Nuts
Popcorn
Potato Chips (Watch for Lard in Ingredients)
Pretzels
Rice Cakes
Salsa
Seeds (Sunflower, Pumpkin, etc.)
Trail Mix

Crackers
Carr's Table Water Crackers
 Original
 With Cracked Pepper
 With Sesame Seeds

Keebler Club Partners
 Original
 Reduced Sodium

Keebler Munch-Em's
 Seasoned Original

Keebler Toasteds Complements
 Onion
 Rye
 Sesame
 Wheat

Keebler Townhouse Classic Crackers

Keebler Wheatables
   50% Reduced Fat
   French Onion
   Low Salt
   Ranch
   Regular

Keebler Zesta Saltine Crackers
   50% Reduced Sodium
   Original
   Unsalted Tops

Nabisco
   Garden Crisps—Vegetable
   Harvest Crisps—5 Grain
   Harvest Crisps—Oat
   Low Sodium Ritz Crackers
   Oysterettes
   Ritz Bits
   Ritz Crackers
   Ritz Crackers with Whole Wheat
   Ritz Sandwiches with Real Peanut Butter
   Sociables
   Uneeda Biscuit
   Waverly
   Wheatsworth

Nabisco Better Cheddars
   Low Sodium
   Original
   Reduced Fat

Nabisco Premium Saltine Crackers
   Fat Free
   Original
   Unsalted Tops
   With Multi-Grain

Nabisco Snack Well's
> Classic Golden Crackers
> Fat-Free Cracked Pepper Crackers
> Fat-Free Wheat Crackers

Nabisco Triscuit
> Deli Style Rye
> Garden Herb
> Low Salt
> Original
> Reduced Fat
> Wheat N' Bran

Nabisco Vegetable Thins

Nabisco Wheat Thins
> Low Sodium
> Multi-Grain
> Original
> Reduced Fat
> Toasted Oat

Old London Melba Snacks
> Mexicali Corn
> Onion
> Sesame
> White

Ralston Purina
> Ry Krisp Natural

Red Oval Farms
> Stoned Wheat Thins

Sunshine Krispy
> Original
> Sunshine Hi-Ho Deluxe
> Unsalted Tops

DESERTS:

<u>Canned fruit</u>
Apples
Applesauce
Berries
Cherries
Citrus Fruit
Cranberry Sauce
Peaches
Pears
Pineapple

<u>Cookies</u>
Delicious
    Skippy Peanut Butter Cookies

Frookie
    Fat-Free All Natural Apple Spice Cookies

Health Valley
    Fat-Free Apricot Delight
    Fat-Free Date Delight

Health Valley Fat-Free Jumbo Fruit Cookies
    Apple Raisin
    Raisin
    Raspberry

Health Valley Fat-Free Mini Fruit Centers
    Apricot
    Raspberry
    Raspberry Apple

Keebler Graham Selects
    Chocolate
    Original

Nabisco
> Oreo's
> Teddy Grahams—Cinnamon

Sunshine
> Hydrox
> Vienna Fingers

Frozen Desserts
Athen Foods
> Baklava

Mrs. Smith's Pies
> Apple
> Deep Dish Apple
> French Silk Chocolate
> Pecan
> Sweet Potato

Pepperidge Farms
> Apple, Blueberry, and Cherry Turnovers
> Peach Dumplings

TAKE-OUT FOODS:

The quickest way to prepare a meal is to take out food. Stop at your local deli counter and pick up potato salad, health salads, hummus, salsa, and other goodies. Ethnic fast food places are also good sources for a quick bite. You can purchase Mexican bean tacos or burritos, vegetable lo mein and/or stir-fried vegetables. Chinese and Thai restaurants are usually happy to prepare any dish without meat if you politely ask. Be sure to request that they do not use fish sauce. Italian Pizza and eggplant subs are also great carry-out items. Some restaurants still fry their food in lard, so you may want to ask some questions before ordering a meal.

Eating Out

Eating out is getting easier and easier for both vegetarians and vegans. If you have a choice, try an ethnic restaurant. Besides Chinese, Mexican, and Italian, good vegetarian eateries (especially in cities) include Indian, Middle Eastern, Thai, Ethiopian, Japanese, and Vietnamese. And, of course, even quick service restaurant chains and truck stops now offer salad bars or other vegetarian choices.

TRUCK STOPS AND SHOPPING CENTERS:
The following is a list of some of the vegetarian items we've found in these places.

Salad bars
Grits
Oatmeal
Hash browns (make sure they are not fried in lard and do not
    contain bacon)
Waffles
Pancakes
English muffins, bagels, etc.
Salads
Vegetarian soups
French fries or onion rings (make sure they are not fried in
    animal fat)
Lettuce, tomato, and vegetable sandwiches
Coleslaw
Eggplant subs
Yogurt
Bean burritos
Veggie burgers
Side orders of vegetables (make sure they do not contain ham)
Pretzels

BOARDWALKS, CARNIVALS, AND PARKS:

Even these havens of typical Americana have items for the vegetarian or vegan.

Sorbet or Italian ices
French fries and onion rings (make sure they are not fried in lard)
Pizza (can be ordered without cheese and with extra vegetables)
Fresh fruit cups
Pretzels with mustard
Fruit shakes
Funnel cakes or fried dough
Corn on the cob
French fried vegetables
Vegetable subs
Popcorn

VEGETARIAN FOOD ON AIRLINES:

If you require a special meal for reasons of health, religion, or personal preference, most airlines will accommodate your needs if you let them know at least 24 hours before your flight departs. We would recommend that you describe your food requirements when making your reservation and then remind the airline again 24 hours before your departure time.

Special meals available may include vegetarian with dairy, vegetarian without dairy or eggs (vegan), diabetic, lowfat, etc. Be specific about what you are requesting. Beware that a lowfat meal probably contains an animal product. Also, quite often airlines forget your special meal request. Therefore, it's best to bring along your own food (especially on long flights).

Vegetarian Menu Items at 72 Fast food Restaurants and Quick Service Chains

Food served in fast food restaurants and quick service chains has become a mainstay in the North American diet. Vegetarianism is also becoming increasingly popular. Where do these two trends meet?

We surveyed over 100 fast food, casual theme dining, and family-style restaurant chains as well as several quick service food chains to find out the current answer to this question. Seventy-two chains responded with intent to show that their establishments can be vegetarian and vegan friendly. We were pleasantly surprised to find out about all of the menu items that are suitable for vegetarians and vegans. In general, we may say that many chains are becoming more health conscious as lowfat or fat-free menu offerings gain popularity. Many of these menu items are vegetarian or can be easily modified to become vegetarian. We are pleased to report that one chain, Subway, with over 13,000 locations worldwide, has earned the right to use the "Five a Day for Better Health" logo of the *Produce for Better Health Foundation*. Subway menu items, several of which are low in fat and all of which contain vegetables, meet the rather strict standards of that organization. We encourage other chains to follow the lead and hope that vegetarian consumers will support those chains which offer healthy, vegetarian meals.

We were happy to learn about the many restaurant chains which are seriously test marketing vegetarian items in selected regions with the hope of adding new items to their national menus. Although we are not throwing all caution to the wind, we can say that a visit to many restaurant chains can make for a satisfying eating experience for vegetarians and vegans alike.

Sometimes, vegetarian or vegan dishes are offered on the menus. Yet even if they are not, it is possible to order menu items without certain ingredients; you just need to ask. For instance, otherwise vegan tacos and pizzas can be ordered without cheese at some restaurant chains that serve these foods. Furthermore, many restaurants would be happy to make specially requested items for guests. For example, Eat n' Park Restaurants, which previously had a vegetable stir-fry on their menu but removed it due to low consumer interest, would prepare the dish on request.

Nevertheless, the vegetarian and vegan should be wary about 'hidden' ingredients (such as gelatin in guacamole or a Danish), or objectionable preparation methods (such as frying hash browns in the same oil used to fry meat/seafood products). It is always best to ask at a particular restaurant. If the given answer is not satisfactory, try calling the corporate headquarters. Ask the manager at the particular restaurant for the phone number.

Likewise, if you are happy with a vegetarian or vegan meal at a restaurant chain or have suggestions on how a restaurant menu can be made more veggie-friendly, please let the manager or corporate headquarters know! Without a demand for vegetarian or vegan options, restaurants remove these offerings from their menus. This happened recently in the case of Denny's which eliminated a vegetarian burger from its menu due to low sales volume.

During the research for this update, we were glad to learn from quality assurance managers of several restaurant chains that many individual consumers contact them for information about their menu offerings. Thus, several chains had already conducted research into their ingredients by contacting their ingredient suppliers. As a result, many responses to us were ready-made. This shows that individuals can and do make a difference.

The most notable example of this occurred in the case of Wendy's. During a phone conversation, a nutrition specialist informed us that an individual recently called to inquire about the gelatin in the Reduced Fat/Reduced Calorie Garden Ranch

Sauce. The nutrition specialist told us that because of this inquiry, she contacted the supplier and requested that the gelatin be taken out of the sauce. The supplier agreed to the request. The new sauce should now be available in Wendy's restaurants.

When you talk to a customer service representative or a quality assurance manager about the sources of an ingredient, such as natural flavors or mono- and diglycerides, you are educating people about the concerns of vegetarians and vegans. You are helping the next person who inquires about that ingredient also.

Many restaurant chains are now exploring the use of ingredients that are at the same time economical and acceptable to all guests, including vegetarians and vegans. For instance, during the research for this update, we learned that almost all restaurant chains use all vegetable shortening for frying. A few use an animal-vegetable shortening blend. Many quality assurance managers told us that the avoidance of animal fats in their recipes and preparation methods was now standard due largely to consumer demand. Although this is not yet a universal preference, we are happy to report it.

The same may be said about the use of animal derived enzymes in cheese. Two cheese suppliers and at least three quality assurance managers at restaurant chains told us that a microbially derived enzyme is currently the enzyme of choice in domestically produced cheeses. We were informed that microbial enzymes are more economical and more efficient at making cheese than their animal counterparts. Keep in mind that animal enzymes are still in use. This is true especially in the case of imported cheeses. Nevertheless, their use in cheese making has been reduced. Of course, we hope that a good-tasting vegan cheese will be an option in the future.

Restaurant chains are realizing the importance of responding to the needs of vegetarians and vegans. For example, Carl's Jr. restaurants asked The VRG to prepare a list of ingredients that are of concern to vegetarians and vegans. They would like to further research the sources of their ingredients so as to serve better their vegetarian and vegan guests. Burger King also asked us to prepare a similar list for the same purpose. Although these requests do not guarantee that restaurant chains will make changes in their ingredients or menus, they represent a first step toward this result.

Some chains are testing vegetarian options in a few of their restaurants. Shoney's, for example, has recently started to test market a vegetarian burger. Burger King has been testing a veggie burger in parts of Canada since October 1996. Burger King continues to have a veggie burger available in its British, Irish, and European restaurants. If you are in any restaurant where a vegetarian or vegan option is being offered, show your support and try it! This is the primary way by which we can keep vegetarian and vegan options on the menus or put them there in the first place. Perhaps one day there will be an all-vegetarian or all-vegan national restaurant chain.

Please use this description of restaurant chains as a guide. Menus and ingredients do change, sometimes suddenly and without well-publicized notification. If you see something which you believe is incorrect, please let us know.

Note: Vegetarian items do not contain meat, fish, or fowl. Vegan foods, in addition to being vegetarian, are free of all animal ingredients including dairy products and eggs.

APPLEBEE'S: Applebee's uses 100% fully hydrogenated vegetable oil to prepare all of its fried items. The same frying equipment and frying surfaces are used for most fried menu items. For example, a grilled cheese sandwich could be prepared on the same surface next to a pastrami sandwich. The same oil is used to fry vegetarian items, such as French fries and mozzarella cheese sticks, and meat products.

Some Applebee's restaurants serve refried beans. The corporate-approved product does not contain lard. Differences may exist at certain franchises, so if you are concerned, ask the restaurant manager.

Applebee's serves several types of baked goods, soups, sauces, and gravies, which may contain animal-derived ingredients. The cheeses at Applebee's may contain animal, vegetable, or microbially derived enzymes. Applebee's stated that vegetable and microbial enzymes are more commonly used, although this may change.

Applebee's offers on its standard menu a Sizzling Vegetable Skillet. This dish consists of red potatoes, zucchini, squash, red and green bell peppers, mushrooms, carrots, and broccoli prepared in lemon and dill flavored butter. The vegetables are first steamed and then further cooked in a skillet. This skillet may be used to prepare meat products, although it is washed in between orders. This entrée may be requested without the butter.

Other standard menu items that may contain, according to Applebee's, "dairy, egg, or other animal-derived ingredients" include the Cheese Quesadilla, Mozzarella Sticks, Onion Peels, Caesar Salad, and the Low-Fat Veggie Quesadilla. The Low-Fat Veggie Quesadilla is composed of fresh mushrooms, red peppers, onion, broccoli, and carrots, along with non-fat shredded cheddar and mozzarella cheeses, in between two wheat tortillas. This menu item is served with fat-free sour cream and shredded lettuce. Note that the Caesar and Pasta Bowl Combo is made with the Caesar salad dressing which contains anchovies.

Applebee's serves various salads, which may be made upon request without meat, poultry, cheese, or eggs. This restaurant chain also offers a salad and steamed vegetable plate, which consists of a house or small Caesar salad followed by a plate of fresh steamed broccoli, carrots, cauliflower, new potatoes, and zucchini. Note that the Caesar dressing contains anchovies.

Available at certain Applebee's Restaurants are the following menu items which may contain, according to Applebee's, "dairy, egg, or other animal-derived ingredients": Parmesan Pizza Sticks, Spinach and Artichoke Dip, Veggie Patch Pizza, Vegetable Stir-Fry, spinach-filled Triple Stack Tortilla, California Vegetable Rollup, Fettuccine Primavera al Pesto, and the Gardenburger®. The Gardenburger® is served with fresh guacamole and

Monterey Jack cheese on a multi-grain roll. Because ingredients in these dishes may vary from restaurant to restaurant, inquire about these entrees at particular Applebee's Restaurants.

Side dishes at this restaurant chain include French fries, new potatoes, baked potatoes, steamed mixed vegetables, coleslaw, and mixed side salad. Like the menu items above, these dishes may contain eggs, dairy, or other animal-derived ingredients.

Applebee's has a child's menu with the following offerings: cheese nachos, cheese pizza, grilled cheese, macaroni and cheese, and pasta marinara. These dishes may contain dairy, eggs, or other animal derived ingredients.

This chain serves a Weekend Brunch. Some menu items that may be appealing to vegetarians include waffles, French toast, cheese/vegetable omelets, spinach and artichoke eggs Benedict, fresh melon, cinnamon rolls, English muffins, and croissants.

Because of Applebee's commitment to providing "World Class Food and Service" to its guests, this restaurant chain is more than happy to modify existing menu items or prepare items upon request in order to accommodate to the greatest degree possible all those with special dietary needs or preferences. Please ask the restaurant manager to assist you.

ARBY'S: The Garden Salad at Arby's contains lettuce, tomato, broccoli, cucumber, shredded carrot, red cabbage, and cheese. This item may be ordered without the cheese. The side salad contains lettuce, tomato, shredded carrot, and red cabbage.

Arby's reports that the following menu items are vegetarian: apple and cherry turnovers, plain and chocolate chip cheesecake, croutons, croissants, blueberry muffins, breakfast biscuits, baked potatoes (plain and broccoli 'n cheddar), and all buns and milkshakes. All of the baked goods contain one or more of the following: honey, non-fat dry milk, and egg. They are all made with vegetable shortening. Note that breakfast items are served in approximately 20% of all Arby's restaurants.

All of the potato products at this restaurant chain are fried in 100% vegetable oil along with the chicken and fish portions.

These menu items include the homestyle fries, the curly fries, the potato cakes, and the French Toastix.

Arby's reports that some of their sauces, gravies, and dressings contain animal derived natural flavors. No further information was available at this time. Arby's could not identify the source of the enzyme used to make their cheeses. They did say that the milkshakes might contain rennet.

According to the most recent brochure, the frozen desserts do not contain gelatin. However, Arby's reports that gelatin may sometimes be an ingredient in these menu items.

There is no MSG in Arby's foods except in the individually labeled packets of ranch dressing.

Arby's is currently evaluating some meatless menu options, such as extending its baked potato line.

AU BON PAIN: Seven varieties of vegetarian bagels are served at Au Bon Pain: plain, sesame, everything, asiago cheese, Dutch apple, cinnamon raisin, and chocolate chip. Of these, the plain, sesame, and cinnamon raisin bagels are vegan. The cream cheese varieties, all made with microbial rennet, include the following: plain, light, sun-dried tomato (light), raspberry (light), vegetable (light), and honey walnut (light).

No animal shortening is used in any of the bread products at Au Bon Pain. Eggs are sometimes used. The Braided Roll contains eggs. All other breads and rolls do not.

The Fresh Mozzarella and Cheese Sandwiches are vegetarian. Among the pastries, the shortbread and all croissants are vegetarian. The following pastries contain eggs: almond croissant, all muffins, all cookies, all Danish, and all scones.

The following soups at Au Bon Pain are vegetarian: Tomato Florentine (contains cheese), Garden Vegetarian, Caribbean Black Bean, Vegetarian Chili, and Cream of Broccoli. The French Onion soup is made with chicken broth.

This bakery and cafe serves salads for lunch and dinner. Both the large and small garden salads consist of two types of lettuce, red cabbage, carrots, tomatoes, cucumbers, and red or green peppers.

All of the sandwiches at Au Bon Pain are made to order, so as long as the ingredients are available, this chain would be happy to accommodate anyone. Nutritional information is available at all restaurants.

AUNTIE ANNE'S: Auntie Anne's is a chain found in many shopping malls, airports, and train stations. They offer a variety of hand-rolled pretzels. The flavored pretzels and dips contain butter. However, although most of their pretzels are flavored with butter, upon request they will make one without butter, and it is vegan. A pretzel ordered here without butter is lowfat. The glaze on the Glazin' Raisin Pretzel contains sugar, butter, and cream cheese. No further information could be provided about the type of cream cheese and sugar used in the glaze.

BASKIN-ROBBINS: Most Baskin Robbins' desserts are vegetarian and some are even vegan. Dairy-free and gelatin-free products include the Ices and Sorbets. Most of their products are also egg-free with the exception of Egg Nog, French Vanilla, Vanilla, and Custard flavors, and those with cookie or cake pieces. Flavors made with miniature marshmallows, however, such as the Rocky Road flavor, contain animal-derived gelatin. The creamy marshmallow flavoring that is a swirl in some of the flavors does not contain gelatin; it is derived from egg whites. The marshmallow topping is also gelatin-free and contains egg whites.

BOJANGLES': The hash browns (borounds) and seasoned fries at Bojangles are cooked in a mix of animal and vegetable oils. This oil has been 'seeded' with the oil that was used to cook chicken in order to impart flavor.

Bojangles offers both marinated coleslaw, which is vegan, and creamy coleslaw, which contains mayonnaise. They serve macaroni and cheese made with Kraft processed American cheese, which contains vegetable-derived enzymes. The mashed potatoes contain natural flavors of an unspecified nature. Fifteen Bojangles' restaurants are test-marketing a new recipe of mashed potatoes that contains sweetened, creamed butter and dry cream.

Bojangles' also serves Cajun pinto beans, which are vegan. The green beans and corn on the cob are also free of animal based seasonings. Bojangles' has recently begun to test-market salads.

The multi-grain roll at Bojangles' contains whey. All of the biscuits contain buttermilk. A breakfast biscuit can be ordered without the meat, egg, and/or cheese upon request. No information was available on the several varieties of pies, which arrive pre-made at the restaurants.

BONANZA: Bonanza restaurants are individually franchised. Because menu items vary among regions and are purchased from a wide listing of manufacturers and distributors, any nutritional evaluation or ingredient listing done on one unit's products may well be invalid for the rest. Vegetable items, salads, and desserts on their salad bars are purchased locally. The national headquarters recommends the use of vegetable oil, but they stated that there is no guarantee that it is used in every restaurant. The restaurant manager will be able to provide you with more information upon request.

BOSTON MARKET: Boston Market reports that the following menu items are vegan: apple cinnamon pie, cranberry walnut relish, fruit salad, steamed vegetables, and zucchini marinara. The following menu items are vegetarian: apple pie, brownies, chocolate chip cookies, cinnamon apples, coleslaw, cornbread, mashed potatoes, oatmeal raisin cookie, potato salad, and butternut squash. The following items may contain animal-derived enzymes: Caesar salad (no chicken), buttered corn, honey wheat & white roll, macaroni & cheese, Mediterranean pasta salad, new potatoes, rice pilaf, creamed spinach, stuffing, and tortellini salad. Boston Market has several different sources for their cheeses, but could not be more specific. Boston Market does not fry its items. Soybean, canola, corn, or cottonseed oils may be used in some of their items. None of the vegetarian/vegan items are cooked in oil that has been used to cook meat or seafood products. Boston Market does not use animal shortening in any of their baked goods. Their gravies contain flavors (such as chicken broth), which have been derived from animal sources. No gelatin is used in the above mentioned menu offerings. Boston Market would be happy to customize sandwiches, but all other items are standardized. This restaurant chain reports that variations in food ingredients may exist in any given restaurant due to locally purchased products and ingredients. Some menu items may not be available in certain restaurants while other restaurants may have regional offerings that could be suitable to vegetarians/vegans.

BRUEGGER'S BAGEL BAKERY: Many of the bagels at Bruegger's are vegan. Exceptions include the sun-dried tomato and spinach herb bagels, which contain Romano cheese, and the jalapeño cheddar bagel, which contains cheddar cheese. The Romano cheese is made with an enzyme of unspecified source. The cheddar cheese is made with microbial rennet. There is egg in the egg bagel, and honey in the honey grain bagel. The everything bagel contains onion, garlic, salt, poppy seed, and sesame. Other varieties that are vegan include chocolate chip, blueberry, and sourdough. Some varieties may not be available at all locations.

Bruegger's offers many varieties of cream cheese. Some of the Light varieties contain microbial rennet while others do not contain any rennet at all. There is no animal rennet in any of the varieties. In some restaurants, the bacon scallion cream cheese contains bacon. It is best to ask at a particular restaurant for verification.

The bagels at Bruegger's may be ordered any way you would like. The customer may choose from a large variety of toppings including lettuce, tomato, onion, sprouts, green pepper, cucumber, light mayonnaise, hot honey mustard, and Dijon mustard.

Bruegger's also serves several vegetarian sandwiches. There is the Leonardo da Veggie Sandwich, which consists of a bagel of your choice, roasted peppers, fresh lettuce, tomatoes, red onion, Muenster cheese, and light herb garlic cream cheese. It is possible to order this sandwich without one or more of these ingredients. The Muenster cheese is made with microbial rennet. Provolone, cheddar, American, or Swiss cheese, all made with microbial rennet, may be available at some restaurants and substituted for the Muenster cheese. The preparation of the roasted peppers may vary from location to location.

Bruegger's also offers a hummus spread. Their garden vegetable spread is a garden vegetable cream cheese, which is available in both full fat and light varieties.

There are several varieties of soups that are vegetarian. Vegan soups include Chile Cilantro, Garden Split Pea, Marcello Minestrone, and Ratatouille. The Gazpacho soup, also vegan, is offered seasonally and only in certain regions. The Velvet Veggie Cheese soup contains milk and American cheese. The cheese is made with a microbial enzyme. The Victory Garden Veggie soup contains Parmesan cheese, made with an enzyme of unknown source. The Creamy Tomato and Idaho Baked Potato soups contain chicken flavoring.

Bruegger's also serves egg sandwiches. The eggs arrive at the bakeries pre-cooked. They contain whole eggs and cream cheese. When ordered, the eggs are rewarmed in an oven. Preparation methods may vary. A disposable paper may be placed between the eggs and meat products during cooking. It is also possible that the eggs would be cooked in a pan containing meat residues. Request that the preparation method avoid contact with meat products if you are concerned.

This restaurant chain also serves cookies and brownies, which contain eggs and dairy. These menu items are purchased locally so it is best to inquire about ingredients at the particular restaurant. The Bruegger's Bar contains whey and sweetened condensed milk, and no egg.

This restaurant chain recently began offering garden salads at some of its locations. The salads come with cheese. Dressings include fat-free Italian, ranch, and French. No further information was available. Inquire at your local Bruegger's for more information.

Each Bruegger's Bakery has ingredient and nutritional information available for customers. Don't hesitate to ask at the restaurant if you would like further detail on any Bruegger's menu item.

BURGER KING: Burger King restaurants sell vegan fries cooked in vegetable shortening. The fries have not been pre-treated with beef fat. This new formula item was introduced in 1997. The fries are cooked in a vat apart from the multi-product vats. The multi-product vat is used to cook hash browns, both regular and mini onion rings (which are otherwise vegan), and French toast sticks as well as meat and seafood products. Burger King uses only vegetable shortening for their fried products.

The hash browns and French toast sticks contain mono- and diglycerides and natural flavors of an unspecified nature. All Burger King buns contain mono- and diglycerides of unspecified nature and/or protease enzymes of an unspecified nature. All buns also contain alpha-amylase, an enzyme of an unspecified nature. The croissants contain skim milk and egg yolks.

Other vegetarian options at Burger King include the garden and side salads. The Garden Salad does contain cheese. Animal or vegetable rennet is used to make all cheeses at Burger King. The Reduced Calorie Light Italian Dressing is vegan. The Bleu Cheese, Ranch, and Thousand Island dressings all contain egg yolk and natural flavors of an unspecified source. Natural flavors of an unspecified source are also contained in the French dressing; otherwise, the French dressing is vegan.

Burger King also offers some vegetarian options on a regional basis. For instance, you may be able to find bagels at some restaurants. Burger King told us that they are Lender's bagels.

We contacted Lender's who said that they use vegetable mono- and diglycerides and synthetic L-cysteine, an amino acid. Lender's declined to send this information to us in writing.

Dutch apple pie is the only pie on the national menu. It contains whey and casein (a milk derivative). Snickers Ice Cream Bar, possibly offered in some Burger King restaurants, contains gelatin.

Since October 1996, Burger King has been successfully marketing a veggie burger in limited areas of Canada, including British Columbia and central Ontario. The principal ingredients are red kidney beans and toasted breadcrumbs. The patties are cooked in all vegetable shortening in a vat used to cook meat and seafood products. No information was available on the bun of this sandwich.

Burger King continues to offer a Spicy Bean Burger in the United Kingdom and Ireland. This burger consists primarily of rolled oats and brown rice. It contains vegetarian mozzarella cheese blend, vegetarian cheddar cheese, egg white, and vegetarian Worcestershire sauce. This burger is microwaved. This burger is supplied by Western Fine Foods and comes in regular and junior sizes. No further information was available on the bun on which the veggie patty is served.

A patty that is very similar to that offered in Canada, containing primarily red kidney beans and toasted bread crumbs, is also offered in Europe. This patty is cooked in the multi-vat along with meat and seafood products.

To urge Burger King to bring a veggie burger to your area and to encourage them to cook the burgers separate from meat and seafood products, call the customer service line at (305) 378-7011.

CARL'S JR.: French fries, onion rings, hash brown nuggets, breaded zucchini, and the CrissCuts at Carl's Jr. are cooked in vegetable oils (corn, cottonseed, and soybean oils). The fries were not pre-cooked in animal fat. However, the fries, onion rings, fried zucchini, and hash browns are cooked in the same oil used to cook meat/seafood products. Their onion rings and breaded zucchini contain whey. The onion rings, hash brown nuggets, and breaded zucchini at Carl's contain natural flavors of an unspecified nature.

Bread products that contain no animal shortening, eggs, or dairy derivatives include the breadsticks, cornmeal bun, plain bun, flour tortilla, and English muffin. Their honey wheat bun contains no eggs, but does contain honey. The raisin bran muffin contains sugar, whole eggs, and whey. All of the bread products except the English and raisin bran muffins, breadsticks, and croutons contain mono- and diglycerides of an unspecified nature.

Carl's has an all-you-can-eat salad bar offering a variety of fresh vegetables and a three-bean salad. Some salad fixings include alfalfa sprouts, broccoli, raisin-sunflower mix, and mush-rooms. Their 'Garden Salad-To-Go'™ is vegetarian when it consists of the salad mix, tomato, cucumber, and grated cheese (made with vegetable rennet). The croutons contain milk, whey, and Parmesan cheese (made with enzymes from an unspecified source).

The Bleu Cheese dressing at Carl's contains egg yolks, sugar and cultured buttermilk solids. The French-Fat-Free dressing contains sugar and modified food starch, both of which may have been processed using animal substances. The Fat-Free Italian dressing also contains these ingredients as well as natural flavor of an unspecified source. The Thousand Island dressing contains sugar, modified cornstarch, and natural flavor as well as egg yolk and Worcestershire sauce (which contains anchovies). The House dressing contains buttermilk powder, egg yolks, MSG, and sugar.

They also offer 'Great Stuff'™ baked potatoes of the following types: plain, broccoli and cheese, and sour cream and chives. Whey-containing margarine is served on request with the plain potato and is automatically put on the other varieties. You may ask for the all-vegetable margarine. The cheese sauce on the broccoli and cheese baked potato is made with vegetable rennet. The sour cream at some Carl's restaurants may contain kosher gelatin or it may be gelatin-free. Inquire about this at the particular Carl's restaurant if you are concerned.

The Swiss and American sliced cheese may contain both animal and vegetable-derived enzymes. However, their shredded cheddar and Jack cheeses and the cheese sauce contain vegetable rennet.

Carl's offers a Breakfast Quesadilla which consists of a flour tortilla, a scrambled egg, grated cheese, and salsa. The tortilla contains L-cysteine of an unspecified source and the salsa contains modified food starch. The grated cheese contains vegetable-derived rennet.

The Breakfast Burrito is made with the same flour tortilla and consists of two whole scrambled eggs, grated cheese, bacon and salsa. It may be ordered without the meat. The cheese is made with a vegetable-derived enzyme and the salsa contains sugar.

They also offer French Toast Dips® which contain mono- and diglycerides, polysorbate 80, lecithin, glycerine, and natural flavor of unspecified sources, as well as non-fat milk. The pancake syrup that is served with the Dips contains sugar and natural flavors of an unspecified source.

Carl's also serves a Sunrise Sandwich®, which consists of a whole egg English muffin, margarine, American cheese, and either bacon or sausage. It may be ordered without the meat. The English muffin is vegan. The margarine on this sandwich contains whey. It is possible to request another variety of margarine, which is all vegetable.

The Scrambled Eggs Breakfast consisting of two whole scrambled eggs, an English muffin, strawberry or grape jelly, margarine, hash brown nuggets, and either bacon or a sausage patty, may also be ordered without meat. The grape jelly is vegan and the strawberry jelly contains sugar. The margarine served with this entree contains whey. Another variety of all-vegetable margarine can be requested. The hash brown nuggets contain natural flavors of an unspecified source.

For dessert, Carl's offers a raspberry parfait, available at the salad bar, which contains gelatin, sugar, polysorbate 60, and fatty acids of unspecified natures. The chocolate cake contains sugar, buttermilk, eggs, modified cornstarch, cream cheese, mono- and diglycerides, and natural flavors. The chocolate caramel crunch moussie contains sugar, modified corn starch, evaporated milk, butter, sodium caseinate, non-fat milk solids, and whey. The moussie also contains the following ingredients of unspecified nature: mono- and diglycerides, natural flavors, lecithin, poly-sorbate 60, and sorbitan monostearate. The chocolate pudding contains skim milk, modified food starch, and mono- and diglycerides. The chocolate chip cookie contains sugar, egg, and butter, and the following ingredients of unspecified natures: lecithin and natural flavoring. Carl's strawberry swirl cheesecake contains cream cheese, whole milk, cream, sugar, non-fat milk solids, whole eggs, whey, gelatin, and the following ingredients of an unspecified nature: mono- and diglycerides, lecithin, modified food starch, natural flavor, and vitamin A palmitate. The cheese Danish contains sugar, whole eggs, sour cream, milk, casein, and the following ingredients of unspecified sources: lecithin, natural flavors, vitamin A palmitate, modified food starch, and mono- and diglycerides.

Carl's also serves shakes. The vanilla shake base, used to make all shakes, contains skim milk, cream, whey, polysorbate 65, and mono- and digylcerides of an unspecified nature.

Carl's Jr. Restaurants will make anything to order. For example, they will gladly serve a 'meatless' burger, which is simply condiments of your choice on a plain bun. Their special sauce contains natural flavoring of an unspecified source. Carl's has a complete ingredients list available for customers at all of their restaurants.

CHECKER'S DRIVE-IN RESTAURANTS: The French fries at Checker's are breaded and may contain beef tallow and/or vegetable oil. The fries are cooked in an animal-vegetable shortening blend. The same oil is used to cook chicken.

Checker's also offers vanilla, chocolate, and strawberry shakes, which contain some butterfat. They serve apple nuggets, which contain a batter similar to that used in the French fries. They are cooked in the same oil as the fries.

One can purchase condiments (including cheese) on a bun at Checker's.

CHI-CHI'S: Chi-Chi's uses all-vegetable oil to prepare their refried beans and other deep-fried items, including meat products. None of their baked goods contain animal shortening at this time. Sometimes eggs, milk, or honey may be used in the baked goods. Suppliers change periodically so Chi-Chi's could not be more specific. A concerned customer may inquire at a particular Chi-Chi's Restaurant for ingredient information.

The cheese at this restaurant chain is primarily made with microbially-derived rennet. However, animal-derived rennet may be used from time to time.

The following menu items are vegan: chips and salsa, Dinner Salad without cheese, Refried Beans without cheese and Guacamole.

The following menu items are vegetarian: Chile Con Queso, Cheese Nachos, Vegetable Chajita, Vegetable Quesadilla, Mexican Fried Ice Cream, and the Apple Chimi. The Chile Con Queso contains a processed cheese blend, red and green peppers, and chile peppers. The Vegetable Chajita consists of sautéed red and green peppers, onions, broccoli, zucchini, squash, and carrots in a vegan tortilla. The margarine used to sauté the vegetables contains whey. The vegetables are prepared in a sauté pan used to cook only vegetables. A guest who would like to make this entree vegan could specially request that the vegetables be steamed rather than sautéed in the whey-containing margarine. Chi-Chi's would try to accommodate such a request.

The Vegetable Quesadilla consists of a blend of melted Monterey Jack and cheddar cheeses, sautéed vegetables (red and green peppers, onions, broccoli, zucchini, squash, and carrots), and a vegan Pico de gallo sauce (chili peppers, onions, tomatoes, cilantro, and other spices), in a flour tortilla. The filled tortilla is lightly grilled on a separate area of a grill surface next to the area where meat products are prepared. The margarine used to sauté the vegetables contains whey.

The Cheese and Onion Enchilada contains cheese, onions, spices, and enchilada sauce in a corn tortilla. The enchilada sauce contains chicken fat. The sauce is contained in the enchilada filling and it is poured over the enchilada. It may be possible at some Chi-Chi's restaurants to order a specially prepared enchilada without the sauce. Guests may ask the restaurant manager.

The Mexican Fried Ice Cream consists of ice cream (made with eggs) which has been coated with corn flakes, cinnamon, and sugar. It is dipped in the same oil used to fry both vegetarian and non-vegetarian foods. A customer may request that this dessert item be served before it has been dipped in the cooking oil. Optional toppings for this menu item include honey, chocolate, and strawberry.

The Apple Chimi consists of apples, cinnamon, and walnuts in a flour tortilla. It is fried in the same oil used to cook both vegetarian and non-vegetarian menu items.

Note that Chi-Chi's Spanish rice contains chicken fat. Also, upon request, Chi-Chi's would prepare a vegetarian bean burrito or bean tostada.

CHILI'S: Chili's offers a wide variety of salads. They serve a garden salad consisting of lettuce, tomatoes, carrots, and other vegetables. They have several salad dressings including House Vinaigrette, which contains natural flavors of an unspecified source. The ranch dressing contains eggs and milk. The honey mustard dressing contains honey. Chili's suggests that those with special dietary concerns may bring their own salad dressing, or simply choose the oil and vinegar as a dressing. Other salads on the menu may be ordered without the meat.

The French fries at Chili's are cooked along with the meat

products. Butter is in the mashed potatoes. Chili's offers a large number of steamed vegetables including squash, broccoli, and corn.

Vegans may order the tortilla with beans. The hot sauce is also vegan.

CHUCK E. CHEESE'S: The pizza at this restaurant chain is made with vegan sauce and dough. The mozzarella and cheddar cheese blend used on the pizzas is made with non-animal rennet. Toppings on the pizza include green peppers, mushrooms, onions, black olives, and tomatoes. The Parmesan cheese is not made with animal-derived rennet.

The salad bar at Chuck E. Cheese's has a wide selection of salad fixings. There are also mayonnaise-based pasta salads and sometimes a three-bean salad. Salad dressings include Thousand Island (contains eggs), ranch and blue cheese (contains dairy), and Italian and fat-free Catalina (both are vegan).

CHURCH'S FRIED CHICKEN: Corn on the cob at Church's may be ordered without butter. The breading used in the fried okra contains whey. This item is fried in vegetable shortening. The French fries, which could be pre-blanched in a product containing beef fat, are also cooked in all vegetable shortening. The meat and non-meat items are cooked in separate fryers. However, the oil is filtered twice a day through the same filter. Therefore, some residual oil from the vat used to cook the meat products could enter into the oil used to cook the non-meat items.

The mashed potatoes at Church's are made from a dry mix, which contains non-fat dry milk and the following ingredients of unspecified source: mono- and diglycerides and natural flavor. The gravy for the mashed potatoes contains chicken fat and rendered beef fat. The coleslaw contains egg white and egg yolk as well as natural flavor of an unspecified source. The biscuits, which contain whey and non-fat dry milk, may be ordered without the honey-butter topping.

There are several desserts at Church's. Except for the natural flavors of unspecified sources, the apple turnover is vegan. The strawberry cream cheese pie contains sweetened condensed milk, cream cheese, and the following ingredients of unspecified source: mono- and diglycerides and natural flavors. The lemon meringue pie contains sweetened condensed milk, vegetable shortening, egg yolk, and egg white. There is no gelatin.

COCO'S: Coco's responded to our survey by saying that they could not respond fully to our questions due to a lack of time and resources but that they would forward to us more information on their menu items at a later date. At this time, Coco's was able to tell us that meat and non-meat items may be fried in the same vegetable oil. Their baked goods may possibly contain animal shortening, honey, eggs, and milk (including milk derivatives). Some of their soups, sauces, gravies, and dressings contain animal-derived natural flavors. Coco's was unable at this time to specify any further.

This restaurant chain reports that the source of the enzyme in their cheese is unknown. They also told us that their frozen desserts might contain gelatin or animal-derived natural color/flavor.

COUNTRY KITCHEN INTERNATIONAL: Country Kitchen offers many salads such as the Southwest Salad, which may be ordered without the meat and/or cheese. It consists of iceberg and leaf lettuce, cabbage, shredded carrots, green onions, tomatoes, cheddar cheese, sour cream, and picante sauce in a wheat tortilla salad shell. The sour cream is purchased locally, so ask the restaurant manager about the ingredients. No further specification was given about the tortilla shell.

This restaurant chain offers a number of side dishes. The rice pilaf contains chicken broth. The mashed potatoes contain milk and butter. There is one or two vegetables offered each day. They are purchased frozen and heated by microwave. The vegetables vary by season and region. They do not contain any animal-derived seasonings and they are not served with cream or cheese sauce.

The French fries at Country Kitchen were not pre-blanched in beef tallow, and they are cooked in 100% vegetable oil. It is possible that meat products could be cooked in the same oil and in the same vat.

Breakfast entrées at Country Kitchen include pancakes and French toast, both of which may be ordered without meat. The pancakes contain eggs and buttermilk. The French toast contains 2% milk and eggs. Although these breakfast items are prepared on a separate area of the grill, away from meat products, it is possible that there would be some residual meat morsels in contact with the vegetarian foods.

Country Kitchen also offers a Garden Omelet, which contains egg whites but is cholesterol-free. It also contains broccoli, mushrooms, onions, tomatoes, and green peppers.

Beverages served at Country Kitchen during all meals include grapefruit, apple, orange, and cranberry juices.

For dessert, there are apple, blueberry, and cherry fruit pies. These are brushed with an egg wash. Country Kitchen also serves baked apple dumplings (no further specification given). In addition, they offer a hot fudge cake served with whipped topping and ice cream. The hot fudge contains dairy products; the cake contains eggs and milk; and the whipped topping contains sodium caseinate, a milk derivative.

CRACKER BARREL: Cracker Barrel wrote us the following letter in response to our request for updated information regarding their vegetarian menu options: "Vegetarianism, as well as, health food issues present us with difficulty in that we do not profess to be a health food or a vegetarian restaurant. I feel a bit hypocritical to respond to your request. Please understand that we do not want to boost such claims.

"We serve traditional hearty country foods that almost always include meat or animal by products in some form. We sometimes offer 'light and lean' food, which usually are soon removed from the menu as a result of low sales. We promise our shareholders that we will sell what our guests want to eat. Please understand our position. We simply don't want to misrepresent ourselves."

DAMON'S, THE PLACE FOR RIBS/DAMON'S CLUBHOUSE: Damon's has a core menu that is national, although individual restaurants may offer other items. They serve salads with a large variety of vegetables and dressings. The Russian, Oil and Vinegar, and Reduced-Calorie Italian dressings are vegan. The Parmesan peppercorn dressing contains egg, buttermilk, and Parmesan cheese made with an enzyme of unspecified source. The Thousand Island dressing contains egg yolks. The Caesar dressing contains cheese and anchovies. The Blue Cheese dressing contains blue cheese, buttermilk, and egg. The No-fat Honey Mustard dressing contains honey and whey powder.

Damon's serves Wholesome & Hearty's Gardenburger, which contains egg whites and cheese. All fried items are prepared in canola oil. The French fries are cooked in the same oil as the chicken. The fries have not been coated. Damon's also serves a vegetable fettuccini, which is made with garlic, oil, and seasonings. The vegetables are roasted in a pan that may have come into contact with meat.

Desserts at Damon's include Chocolate Decadence (which contains ice cream and whipped cream), Oreo Cookie Pie, Apple Cranberry Crumble (which contains butter) and cheese-cake.

DEL TACO: All menu items at Del Taco are lard-free. They use vegetable oil (containing one or more of the following oils: palm, sunflower, cottonseed, corn, or soybean oil) to fry the chips. The French fries, which do not contain any suspicious natural flavors, are cooked in vegetable shortening. The fries and chips are cooked apart from the meat products. However, it is possible that the shell used in the tostada salad has been cooked along with the meat products.

The seasoning used in the beans contains "meat type flavor." One ingredient is natural flavor of an unspecified nature. The rice seasoning contains chicken broth.

The natural cheddar and pepperjack cheeses at Del Taco are made with microbial enzymes. The soft cheese used on the burgers is made with animal-derived rennet. The green chili sauce is vegan and all the hot sauces (available in small packets) appear to be vegan. The secret sauce contains whole eggs.

The shakes at Del Taco contain milk, skim milk, and mono- and diglycerides of an unspecified nature. The chocolate and strawberry shakes are the same as the vanilla shake, with only the addition of chocolate and strawberry syrup, respectively.

DENNY'S: Vegan options at Denny's include the following: Cereal Combo (with grits or oatmeal and English muffin or bagel), fresh fruit, hashed browns, baked potato, side salad (with light Italian, reduced French or Oriental dressing and without cheese or croutons), and Dutch apple pie. Note that Denny's product specification for their English muffin and bagel do not list milk or milk derivatives. However, the bread products are purchased locally and customers should check the labels to confirm that there is no milk or milk derivatives. Request dry bread products in order to avoid the buttery spread. Note that the hashed browns are cooked on a grill with fresh soybean oil although there could be residues on the grill left from meat products.

Lacto-vegetarian options include the following: pancakes, biscuits, cold cereals with milk, 'covered/smothered' hashed browns (covered and smothered in cheddar cheese, onions, and a gravy containing sausage), deluxe grilled cheese, vegetables (corn, peas, broccoli), and mozzarella cheese sticks. Note that soybean oil is used for all fried items. French fries are prepared in 'day 1' (unused) oil. Onion rings and cheese sticks are prepared in the same oil in which chicken, beef, or fish have been fried.

Lacto-ovo vegetarian menu offerings include waffles, French

toast, veggie-cheese omelet, blueberry muffin, two-egg breakfast, side Caesar salad, Texas toast, assorted pies, cakes, and ice cream.

Although some items, such as breads, are purchased locally (and, so, may vary in ingredients), Denny's product specifications for baked goods indicate that the following should be used: vegetable shortening (canola, soybean, cottonseed, or corn oils); honey (in their dinner roll, cheesecake, and French silk pie); eggs (in their Texas toast, French bread, hamburger bun, and dinner roll as well as in all cakes and pies except the Dutch apple pie); milk and milk derivatives (in all of their breads, pies and cakes except the following: rye, multi-grain, sub roll, flour tortilla, English muffin, bagel, apple pie, cherry pie, pecan pie).

None of the soups at Denny's are vegetarian. The following salad dressings contain eggs: blue cheese, French, Thousand Island, honey mustard, Caesar. The following dressings contain milk or milk derivatives: creamy Italian, blue cheese, Thousand Island, Ranch, honey mustard, and Caesar. Light Italian, reduced French, and Oriental dressings contain neither eggs nor milk/milk derivatives.

The cheeses at Denny's may contain enzymes that are either animal or microbial in origin. Gelatin is contained in the following products: Parmesan cheese, lemon meringue pie, and the vegetable beef soup. The rice pilaf contains chicken broth. Denny's regular French fries contain beef fat. Although their seasoned fries do not contain beef fat, they do contain natural flavors of an unspecified nature.

Denny's is very open to accommodating people with special dietary requests. For example, the meats used in their breakfast Slams could be substituted with fruit or tomato slices. Customers should ask their server about leaving off specific ingredients (such as cheese or mayonnaise) that do not meet with the individual's dietary restrictions.

Due to a low sales volume, Denny's discontinued its vegetarian burger. If you would like to call Denny's to ask them to bring it back, call their customer service line at (800) 7-DENNYS.

DOMINO'S: All three types of pizza crusts at Domino's contain whey. Only the hand-tossed crust contains 'flavorings' and mono- and diglycerides of an unspecified nature. L-cysteine, an amino acid that functions as a dough conditioner, is used in the crusts. Its source may vary. Soybean oil is the only type of oil used at Domino's.

The enzymes used in the cheese at Domino's are of microbial origin. The sauce contains no obvious meat flavorings, such as chicken broth or beef fat, although Domino's cannot offer any guarantee that the 'natural flavoring' in the sauce is all-vegetable. Domino's gives no specifications to its suppliers that animal-derived ingredients are not to be used even when alternative sources of the ingredients are available.

Domino's does offer salads that are vegan. They use Marzetti salad dressings. The Ranch dressing contains egg yolks; the French dressing contains natural flavors of an unspecified source; and the Italian and Lite Italian dressings are vegan. A few Domino's restaurants offer subs, all of which are meat-based. There may be whey in the sub roll.

EAT'N PARK: Vegetarian options at Eat'n Park include the Garden Burger (which has cheese in it) and a non-advertised vegetarian stir-fry, which can be requested. Due to lack of sales, the stir-fry is no longer on the menu. The stir-fry consists of a variety of vegetables. Depending on the consumer's request, the stir-fry may be cooked with or without oil. The oil is unused, butter-flavored cottonseed oil. The butter flavoring is synthetic. Eat'n Park also offers numerous salad bar items that are suitable for vegetarians and vegans including a three-bean salad. Their pasta salads contain mayonnaise. The French fries may be cooked in oil that had been used to cook meat/seafood products. The French fries were not pre-cooked in beef fat, although they were pre-blanched in canola or soybean oil. Animal products are not used in their breads and rolls, although milk and eggs are used in the sweetened items, such as cakes. For dessert, Eat'n Park offers fruit cups, including year round fresh strawberries.

EL CHICO'S: Canola oil is used for frying at this chain. The all-vegetable French fries are cooked apart from meat products. The taco salad and tostada shells, both of which contain lard, are also cooked in this manner. The taco salad may be ordered without meat.

The beans at El Chico's are refried in animal-vegetable shortening. The flour tortilla contains lard and the Monterey Jack and cheddar cheeses are made with animal-derived rennin. The guacamole does not contain gelatin.

EL POLLO LOCO: The French fries, tortilla chips, and tostada shells are fried in soybean oil at El Pollo Loco. These otherwise vegan items are cooked along with chicken taquitos. The smokey black beans are seasoned with ham. They also contain honey and natural flavor of an unspecified source.

The flour, spinach-flavored and tomato-flavored tortillas are vegan. The BRC burrito contains cheese, although it may be ordered without it. The cheese at El Pollo Loco may contain either animal-derived or microbially-derived rennet. Any meat-containing burrito, like all meat-containing menu items at El Pollo Loco, may be ordered without the meat.

Among the many side dishes served at El Pollo Loco, the following are vegan: pinto beans, corn-on-the-cob, cucumber salad, spiced apples, and guacamole. The hot sauce, salsa, and Italian dressing are also vegan. The Spanish rice and Fiesta Corn, which contain margarine, appear to be vegan. No further information was available on the ingredients in the margarine (which sometimes contains whey).

The mashed potatoes and flan at this restaurant chain contain milk. The Southwest dressing in the Southwest coleslaw and on the Southwest Wrap, as well as the potato salad, contain eggs and natural flavors of unspecified natures. The broccoli slaw and rainbow pasta salad contains eggs. The macaroni and cheese dish contains milk and eggs. Except for the Italian dressing, all of the salad dressings at El Pollo Loco contain eggs and natural flavors of unspecified natures. The Ranch, Bleu Cheese, and

Caesar dressings also contain milk. The Caesar dressing contains anchovies.

The Crispy Green Beans at El Pollo Loco contain bacon. The Honey Glazed Carrots contain dairy and honey. The Fiesta Cornbread Stuffing contains chicken and natural flavors of an unknown source, and the chicken gravy contains chicken.

Gelatin is an ingredient in the lite sour cream and in the Lime Parfait at El Pollo Loco.

Ingredient information was unavailable for the churros and the Fosters Freeze. A concerned customer may inquire about these items at a particular El Pollo Loco. However, churros are cooked in the same soybean oil used to fry the chicken taquitos.

El Pollo Loco would be happy to accommodate vegetarians by eliminating dressings, sauces, cheese, and/or meat from any menu item requested.

FUDDRUCKERS: The newest addition to Fuddruckers' menu is the Vegetarian Fuddwrapper. It is currently being offered only in a selected number of restaurants. Fuddruckers hopes that this menu item will be available in all restaurants in 1998.

The Fuddwrapper consists of a lightly seasoned medley of vegetables, rice, and mozzarella cheese inside of a soft tortilla. There are tomato, spinach, whole wheat, and cheese tortillas. Tyson Foods, the supplier of the tortillas, reports that the tomato, spinach, and whole wheat tortillas are vegan. The cheese tortilla contains cheese and cheese flavoring. The enzyme used to make the cheese is of an unknown source. There are onions, tomatoes, green peppers, mushrooms, zucchini, and sweet potatoes that have been marinated in vegetable oil and herb seasoning. They are then grilled on a surface to which a light coating of vegetable oil has been applied. The vegetables are cooked apart from meat products on a special section of the grill. If a customer is concerned about contamination from meat residues, he or she may ask that the vegetable section of the grill be cleaned again. The white rice in the Fuddwrapper has been boiled and contains a small quantity of added turmeric and parsley. The mozzarella cheese has been made with an enzyme of unknown source.

Fuddruckers also serves a taco salad that is served with cheese. No further information on this menu item was available. French fries at this restaurant chain are fried in all vegetable shortening in a vat apart from meat products. The onion rings are also fried in this manner.

Fuddruckers has a fixins' bar. A vegetarian should be able to order condiments and/or cheese on a bun with any of the large selection of items at the fixins' bar. The Pico de Gallo sauce is chopped tomatoes and onions with seasoning. The bun contains egg.

On the menu at many Fuddruckers are Caesar and garden salads. The Caesar salad consists of romaine lettuce, grated cheese, and croutons. The Caesar dressing is a Hellman's product. The Garden salad is served with a cheddar sauce.

Dessert items at this restaurant chain include brownies, cookies, and Kellogg's Rice Krispie treats. The latter contain butter and marshmallow, which is made with gelatin.

One or two franchise restaurants in Texas serve a veggie burger, which is doing rather well. Tell the manager at a Fuddruckers near you that you would like this vegetarian option on the menu at all Fuddruckers.

GIOVANNI'S PIZZA: Giovanni's pizza offers pizza, spaghetti, lasagna, and a wide variety of salads including garden, chef, and antipasto salads. The choice of provolone or mozzarella cheese is offered. The two may also be mixed. Giovanni's was unable to specify the type of enzyme used in their cheeses. The dough and pizza sauce are vegan. Vegan pizza toppings include banana peppers (mild, yellow chili peppers), olives, onions, green peppers, and mushrooms.

The spaghetti sauce and lasagna have meat in them. Provolone and mozzarella cheeses are used in the lasagna.

Giovanni's salads, which normally contain meat, may be ordered without the meat. Their dressings, including Thousand Island, Italian, blue cheese, and buttermilk, are made by Kraft.

Giovanni's does not serve dessert.

GODFATHER'S PIZZA: Godfather's Pizza offers a vegetarian specialty pizza, which may be ordered without the cheese to make it a vegan pizza. The toppings on this pizza are the following: mushrooms, black olives, green peppers, onions, and tomatoes. The cheeses used on the pizzas are mozzarella and cheddar. These cheeses are made with microbial enzymes. Parmesan cheese is offered as an extra topping and is on certain specialty pizzas. Godfather's was unable to give further specification on its ingredients. The pizza dough is vegan. The two pizza sauces, original and taco, are vegan.

Several types of breadsticks are offered at Godfather's. Their own breadsticks contain dry milk. Those that are pre-made could have a wide variety of ingredients, depending on the manufacturer. Local bakeries may make some breadsticks.

Some Godfather's restaurants may serve salads. Offerings and dressings depend on the local restaurant. Likewise, soups and desserts may be offered in particular restaurants. One possible dessert, the streusel, contains white and brown sugars. Otherwise, it is vegan. Inquire at particular Godfather's restaurants about the ingredients in any menu item.

GOLD STAR CHILI: Gold Star Chili serves a tossed salad composed of lettuce, tomatoes, onions, jalapeño, peppers, olives, shredded cheese, and garlic bread. They offer no vegetarian chili or veggie dogs. They do serve nacho chips. Some Gold Star Chili restaurants offer waffle fries. These fries contain beef fat and/or partially hydrogenated soybean oil and/or canola oil.

GOLDEN FRIED CHICKEN: Golden Fried Chicken restaurants serve pasta and fruit salads. The pasta salad contains mayonnaise. The carrot raisin salad is vegan. They also serve coleslaw dressing, which contains mayonnaise.

The pinto and green beans at Golden Fried Chicken contain

bacon and bacon grease. The French fries are coated with a batter of unknown nature. The fries are cooked in an animal-vegetable shortening blend apart from the chicken.

The biscuits at Golden Fried Chicken contain buttermilk and the yeast-risen rolls come pre-made to all the restaurants. Further specification on the rolls could not be given.

For dessert, Golden Fried Chicken serves chocolate chip cookies (which contain milk), bread pudding (which contains eggs and milk), and apple turnovers (which are fried in the animal-vegetable shortening blend).

GREAT STEAK AND FRY COMPANY: This restaurant chain has a vegetarian sandwich on its menu. The sandwich consists of Swiss and provolone cheese (the enzymes in the cheeses are of unspecified sources), onions, mushrooms, green peppers, cucumbers, and black olives. A choice of dressings, including ranch, Italian, lite French, and French, is offered. These are all Marzetti dressings. The sandwich may be ordered without the cheese. The roll is a Pillsbury Rudi® roll; no further specifications could be given by either the restaurant chain or by the food suppliers.

The Great Steak and Fry Co. also serves French fries. They are fresh-cut and pre-blanched in peanut oil. Only the fries are prepared in oil at this restaurant chain.

Side items that are available include baked potatoes, which may be requested plain, or served with broccoli, broccoli and cheese sauce, or with mixed vegetables in an all-vegetable broth. Some restaurants do not serve potatoes.

Salads are served at all Great Steak and Fry Co. restaurants. There is a plain side salad, with optional Swiss, provolone, or cheddar cheese. There is also a chef's salad that includes hot peppers, cucumbers, and olives. It may be ordered without the meat. No desserts are offered at this restaurant chain.

HARDEE'S: The French fries at Hardee's are made of all-vegetable ingredients. The Crispy Curls contain whey. These menu items are fried in the same oil that is used to fry the meat and seafood products. The mashed potatoes contain natural flavoring of an unspecified source. The coleslaw contains egg yolks.

It is possible to order cheese and/or condiments on a bun at this restaurant chain. Hardee's serves shredded cheddar, shredded Monterey Jack, sliced American, and sliced Swiss cheeses. Both plant and animal derived enzymes are used to make these cheeses.

Hardee's sourdough bread and specialty bun are vegan. The seeded bun contains whey.

Hardee's no longer offers a garden salad as a menu item. This chain does offer a vegan side salad consisting of lettuce, tomatoes, cucumbers, carrots, and purple cabbage. The Thousand Island dressing contains egg yolk and natural flavors of an unspecified source. The fat-free French dressing contains yogurt and skim milk. The house dressing contains buttermilk and egg yolks. No Italian or oil-and-vinegar dressing is available.

The breakfast biscuits at Hardee's contain whey. There are an apple cinnamon raisin biscuit, and an egg and cheese biscuit. The latter may be ordered without either the egg and/or the cheese. American cheese is used in this sandwich.

Some Hardee's restaurants serve pancakes. The pancakes contain buttermilk and eggs. The hash rounds are fried potatoes with natural flavoring of an unspecified source. They are cooked in the same oil used to prepare meat products. Gelatin-free yogurt containing natural flavors of an unspecified source is served.

In the summer of 1997, pita pockets were test-marketed at selected Hardee's restaurants. No further information is available at this time.

HOT STUFF PIZZA: The pizza dough at Hot Stuff is coated with butter flavor oil, which is enhanced with natural butter flavor. Otherwise, the dough is vegan. The mozzarella cheese ingredient statement does not list enzymes at all. The pizza sauce and breadsticks are vegan. No animal fat is used in any of the menu items at Hot Stuff Pizza. The egg rolls contain pork.

HOULIHAN'S: This restaurant chain offers a vegan pasta dish consisting of rigatoni and marinara sauce. The sauce contains oven-roasted vegetables including broccoli, onion, mushrooms, sun-dried tomatoes, and spices.

The tomato bruschetta consists of vegan bread that has been brushed with garlic and olive oil and then toasted. The bread is topped with tomatoes and Romano cheese (made with a vegetable enzyme). This entrée may be requested without the cheese.

Houlihan's offers a variety of salads on its menu. Although there is no garden salad, any salad may be ordered without the meat. They have a vegan oil and vinegar dressing and several vegetarian dressings such as honey and lime citrus, and a Chinese dressing containing sugar, lime, and soy sauce. The Caesar dressing contains anchovies.

The French fries are all vegetable. They are cooked in canola oil apart from meat/seafood products. The mushrooms at Houlihan's are cooked in oil used to fry chicken. The vegetable soup is made with beef base.

Since October 1997, Houlihan's has been offering a quesadilla. It contains goat cheese (made with an animal enzyme), fresh spinach, peppers, onions, and grilled mushrooms. The mushrooms are cooked on a 450-degree grill surface. The grill is segmented into separate parts for vegetables, meats, and seafood.

For dessert, there is apple pie, which is made in-house. The pie may be served with or without ice cream. A different-flavor vegan sorbet is offered each day.

Houlihan's is test-marketing their own vegan burger in three of their restaurants. It contains couscous, black beans, carrots, onions, and barbecue sauce. The roll contains eggs or dairy.

HOWARD JOHNSON'S RESTAURANTS: Howard Johnson's serves Wholesome & Hearty's Gardenburger®, which contains egg whites and cheese. It is served on a Kaiser roll. The Gardenburger® may be substituted for meatballs in the spaghetti and meatballs entree when requested. There is no meat base in the spaghetti sauce.

Since May 1997, Howard Johnson's has offered a vegetable roll-up sandwich, which replaced the veggie pocket sandwich previously offered. The veggie roll-up contains stir-fried veggies accompanied by fajita-seasoned sour cream, iceberg lettuce, tomatoes, and alfalfa sprouts, all in a tortilla shell. No further information on the veggie roll-up was available at this time.

This restaurant chain also offers a Caesar salad. According to a restaurant representative, the Caesar dressing does not contain anchovies. They also offer garden salads.

The French fries are cooked in 100% vegetable oil. They have not been pre-blanched with a beef product. Seafood products are cooked along with the French fries.

Breakfast entrees are also available at Howard Johnson's. The eggs are grilled in vegetable oil where meat products had been prepared. No further information was available on the other breakfast foods such as breads, hotcakes, and potato cakes.

Desserts at Howard Johnson's include ice cream, apple pie, carrot cake, brownie sundaes, and cheesecake. No further information on these menu items was available at this time.

JACK IN THE BOX: The following information is taken from Jack in the Box's brochure, Jack's Nutrition Facts, effective as of April 1997.

Bread products at Jack in the Box contain many ingredients of unspecified source. The gyro bread, hamburger buns, sourdough bread, thick pita bread, and wheat bun contain mono- and diglycerides and enzymes. L-cysteine is listed as an ingredient in the thick pita bread. The Philly roll contains whey. The sesame seed bun contains mono- and diglycerides. However, the pita bread is vegan. All of their cheeses contain enzymes of an unspecified nature.

The French fried potatoes and onion rings contain whey and are cooked in their shortening blend, which is vegan. The onion rings also contain buttermilk powder and non-fat dried milk. The malted barley flour used to make the onion rings contains sulfites. The potato wedges are vegan. The seasoned curly fries contain natural flavors of an unspecified source and are cooked in the vegan shortening blend.

The breakfast offerings at Jack in the Box include buttermilk pancakes, which are made with buttermilk, whey, eggs, and natural flavors of an unspecified source. The pancake, grape, strawberry, and cappuccino syrups are vegan. The creamer contains milk or skim milk. The croissant contains enzymes, L-cysteine hydrochloride, (an amino acid which functions as a dough conditioner), and mono- and diglycerides of unspecified sources. Jack in the Box hash browns contain natural flavoring of an unspecified source.

Jack in the Box also offers a Stuffed jalapeño, which consists of fried jalapeño peppers stuffed with cheddar, Monterey Jack, and cream cheeses. This item is cooked in vegetable shortening. Its enzymes, mono- and diglycerides, and natural flavors are of unspecified sources. Jack in the Box also offers an egg roll containing pork.

Jack in the Box has many sauces for its entrées. The teriyaki sauce contains brown sugar (possibly filtered through a cow bone charcoal filter) but is otherwise vegan. The barbecue dipping sauce, the spicy barbecue sauce, and the sweet and sour dipping sauce contain brown sugar and natural flavors of an unspecified nature. The buttermilk dipping sauce contains buttermilk solids, egg yolk, non-fat dried milk, natural flavors of an unspecified source, and MSG. The hot sauce packet and taco sauce contains MSG and is vegan. The soy sauce packet, malt vinegar packet, and salsa are vegan. The sour cream packet contains milk, cream, and natural flavors of an unspecified source. The tartar sauce contains egg and natural flavor of an unspecified source. The mayo-onion sauce contains egg yolks and natural flavors of an unspecified source. The secret sauce contains egg yolks and Worcestershire sauce (which contains anchovies).

Jack in the Box also offers a side salad, which contains cheddar cheese. Their blue cheese dressing contains enzymes, disodium inosinate and disodium guanylate of unspecified sources, as well as egg yolks. The buttermilk house dressing contains egg yolks, buttermilk, natural flavors of an unspecified source, and MSG. The Caesar dressing contains anchovies and white wine. The French dressing contains honey and natural flavors of unspecified sources. The Italian Low Calorie dressing contains natural flavors of an unspecified source and sugar. The Thousand Island dressing contains egg yolks and natural flavors of an unspecified source. The croutons contain butter flavor, which is in part composed of unspecified natural flavors.

Jack in the Box has many dessert offerings. The apple turnover is vegan. Note that the evaporated apples used in it have been treated with sulfites. The carrot cake contains eggs, cream cheese, whey, and the following ingredients of unspecified sources: mono- and diglycerides, lecithin, poly-sorbate 80, and natural flavoring. The double fudge cake contains sugar, buttermilk, eggs, cream cheese, whey, and the following ingredients of unspecified source: mono- and diglycerides and lecithin. The Oreo cookie crumbs contain sugar and whey. The cheesecake at Jack in the Box contains gelatin.

JB'S RESTAURANTS: Some JB's serve Wholesome & Hearty's Gardenburger®. There is a salad bar. Several soups are offered including cream of potato, cream of broccoli, and tomato Florentine. No further information was available on the vegetarian menu items at JB's.

KFC: KFC uses only soybean oil containing up to 5% cottonseed oil for all of its frying. The potato wedges and French fries are cooked in oil used to prepare chicken.

There are two breads, both containing dairy and egg products but no animal shortening, which are served at this restaurant chain. Other vegetarian options include mayonnaise-based coleslaw, potato salad (which contains egg), mashed potatoes containing butter and milk, and corn on the cob. The gravy served with the mashed potatoes contains meat flavoring. A customer may request the potatoes without the gravy. The corn is served with butter although it can be requested without it. There are packets of a spread which can be used instead (ingredients should be on the packet). The macaroni and cheese is made with cheese containing "suitable enzymes." No further information was available on the enzyme.

About 20% of all KFC restaurants have an all-you-can-eat buffet where hot vegetables are served. Meat flavorings may be used, but this varies from restaurant to restaurant. Inquire about this if you are concerned. At the buffet is a wide selection of salad fixings. Some stores may offer a garden salad that is vegan.

The green beans, mean greens, red beans and rice, and barbecue baked beans all contain meat or meat flavorings. Side dishes vary from restaurant to restaurant, but those mentioned here are served in almost all KFC restaurants.

For dessert, this chain serves Little Bucket Parfaits. The chocolate parfait may contain lard. Some of the other flavors, such as lemon or strawberry, may contain animal-derived mono- and diglycerides. Gelatin is not an ingredient in the parfaits although all of the parfaits contain eggs and dairy products.

LITTLE CAESARS: Little Caesars uses microbial rennet in their pizza cheeses. Their dough and tomato sauce are vegan. Other vegan items include the Crazy Sauce® and Crazy Bread® without Parmesan cheese. The Parmesan cheese may contain animal rennet. The pizza toppings available at Little Caesars include mushrooms, onions, green peppers, tomato slices, black olives, pineapple, and hot peppers. Little Caesars would be happy to prepare menu items on request.

You may contact Little Caesars for their Vegetarian Guide at the following address: Corporate Communications, 2211 Woodward Ave., Detroit, MI 48201-3400.

LONG JOHN SILVER'S: All their fried foods are prepared in 100% soybean oil. Non-meat items, such as French fries and hushpuppies, are fried in the same oil used to cook the meat and seafood products.

In November 1996, Long John Silver's introduced an item known as a Wrap. The wrap itself is made of corn. The contents include fish, chicken, or shrimp along with the following ingredients: rice, lettuce, tomatoes, crumblies (pieces of fried batter cooked in the oil used to cook meat/seafood products), a white sauce, and a flavoring sauce (which could be tartar or picante sauce, or a salad dressing such as Caesar or ranch dressing). It is possible to make a vegan Wrap by ordering it without the meat/seafood, crumblies, and white sauce, but with the picante sauce.

The following menu items at Long John Silver's contain eggs and dairy: hushpuppies, cheesesticks, Fat-Free Ranch, Ranch, and Caesar dressings, and the white sauce used in the Wraps.

The sandwich buns, coleslaw, and Thousand Island dressing contain eggs. All desserts at Long John Silver's contain milk or milk products.

Some restaurants serve green beans, but the seasoning used contains meat flavorings.

MANCHU WOK: Manchu Wok serves stir-fried mixed vegetables. The vegetables include broccoli, baby corn, carrots, mushrooms, and cabbage cooked in canola oil. The fried rice is made with vegetable oil and a sauce on which there was no further information. The chow mein is made with egg noodles. It also contains bean sprouts, carrots, and celery. The egg roll wrapping contains egg. The egg roll stuffing is vegan. This Oriental restaurant chain does not serve tofu. Some Manchu Woks may prepare dishes upon special request if the particular restaurant is not too busy.

MANHATTAN BAGEL CO.: This bagel chain does have a standard menu although some differences may exist from restaurant to restaurant. The menu is complete with ingredient listings and nutritional information given for each variety of bagel. With the exception of the jalapeño cheddar and cheddar cheese bagels, which contain cheddar cheese, and the egg bagel, which contains eggs, the bagels are vegan. The dough conditioner for the bagels is a soybean extract.

The cheeses at Manhattan Bagel are all made with microbial enzymes. This includes the cheddar, Swiss, American, and provolone cheeses as well as the cream cheese. Manhattan Bagel also offers a number of gourmet spreads, all containing cream cheese, including vegetable, raisin & walnut, scallion, strawberry, and sun-dried tomato varieties. This chain offers a pizza bagel made with mozzarella cheese and all-vegetable tomato sauce.

Manhattan Bagel also serves eggs on a bagel, with or without any variety of cheese, all day long. Some restaurants use grills to prepare the eggs. Other restaurants use convection or microwave ovens. If a grill is used, it is possible that there would be some meat residues or oil on the grill where the eggs are cooked.

This restaurant chain also offers bialys, a flattened onion and poppy seed bagel, which is vegan.

MAZZIO'S PIZZA: The thin and original crusts at Mazzio's are vegan. The deep pan crust contains non-fat dry milk. The pizza sauce is vegan. 100% whole milk mozzarella cheese, made with microbial rennet, is used. The four-cheese blend pizza consists of Monterey Jack, mozzarella, provolone, and cheddar cheeses. Microbial rennet is used in all of these cheeses. It is possible to order a cheeseless pizza.

Pizza toppings at this restaurant chain include green peppers, black and green olives, pineapple, jalapeño peppers, onions, tomatoes, and mushrooms.

Some varieties of pasta are vegan. Certain other varieties contain eggs. Vegan marinara sauce made with olive oil is served with the pasta. The Alfredo sauce contains butter, cream, and Parmesan and Romano cheeses. No further information is available on the enzymes used to make these two cheeses.

All the calzone rings and sandwiches at Mazzio's Pizza are meat-based. It is not possible to order them without the meat.

Mazzio's has a salad bar. There is a three-bean salad among the offerings at some locations. The Italian and French dressings are vegan. Except for the honey, the honey mustard dressing is vegan. The blue cheese, Thousand Island, ranch, and lite ranch dressings are cream-based.

The breadsticks at Mazzio's are made with the deep pan dough; thus, they contain non-fat dry milk. The marinara dipping sauce is vegan.

McDONALD'S: McDonald's wrote to us in April 1996 that in Canada, their French fries are parfried and cooked "in a blend of beef tallow and cottonseed oil," both by their supplier and at the restaurant. McDonald's also then wrote "[t]he primary cooking oils used in McDonald's restaurants around the world include cottonseed, tallow, soybean, and corn oils." In the United States, both the parfrying process by their supplier and the preparation at the restaurant is done in vegetable oil. The fries are parfried in soybean oil and later cooked in a blend of corn and soybean oils.

In February 1997, McDonald's informed us by telephone that the natural flavor in their French fries is a "beef product." At that time, they declined to send us this information in writing. In July 1997, McDonald's sent us a fax stating that "[t]he natural flavor used in French fries is from an animal source." McDonald's reports that the fries are cooked in vegetable oil apart from the meat/seafood products. According to their February 1997 Nutrition Facts brochure, the French fries are cooked in a blend of soybean and corn oils, TBHQ (a synthetic antioxidant), citric acid, dimethylpolysiloxane (a synthetic antifoaming agent), and natural flavor.

Many McDonald's restaurants would be happy to prepare upon request one of their sandwiches without meat. The Deluxe roll contains buttermilk solids, animal-derived natural flavors, and vegetable emulsifiers and mono- and diglycerides. The regular, Quarter Pounder, and Big Mac buns contain vegetable mono- and diglycerides and emulsifiers. Both the processed American cheese and the processed, shredded cheddar cheese contain enzymes of either an animal or synthetic source.

The Arch Deluxe sauce contains white wine, eggs, and sugar. The Big Mac and tartar sauces contain egg yolks, sugar, and vegetable-derived natural flavors. The Honey Mustard sauce contains white wine, egg yolks, sugar, honey, and vegetable derived natural flavors.

McDonald's offers a garden salad composed of lettuce, tomatoes, and carrots. The Caesar and Red French Reduced Calorie dressings contain Worcestershire sauce (which contains anchovies). The Fat-Free Herb Vinaigrette contains vegetable derived natural flavors and modified food starch of a synthetic source. The Ranch dressing contains whey, sugar, egg yolks, and animal derived buttermilk flavor with other animal-derived natural flavors. The croutons contain vegetable derived natural flavors.

The shakes at McDonald's are made with whole milk, sucrose, non-fat milk solids, and cream. The chocolate and strawberry flavored shake syrups contain sugar. The vanilla shake syrup also contains sugar as well as vegetable natural flavor.

For breakfast, McDonald's serves Egg McMuffins, which can be ordered without the meat. The English muffin contains vegetable mono- and diglycerides. The Bacon, Egg & Cheese Biscuit can be ordered without the bacon. The Buttermilk Biscuit contains sugar, cultured low-fat buttermilk, and vegetable mono- and diglycerides. The biscuit dressing, used to prepare the biscuits, contains animal-derived natural flavors.

McDonald's also offers hash browns for breakfast. The hash browns contain animal-derived natural flavors and are cooked in an oil blend that contains animal-derived natural flavors. The hash browns are cooked apart from the meat/seafood products.

The hotcakes contain sugar, whey, eggs, vegetable mono- and diglycerides, and vegetable natural flavors. The hotcake syrup also contains sugar and vegetable derived natural flavor. The margarine contains whey and the following ingredients of vegetable source: mono- and diglycerides, lecithin, and vitamin A palmitate. The grape jam and strawberry preserves contain sugar.

Also on the breakfast menu is a breakfast burrito composed of a flour tortilla, meat, and green chilies. Upon request it may be ordered without the meat. The tortilla contains whey. Depending on the location, the tortillas may also contain non-fat dry milk. The mono- and diglycerides and L-cysteine may be derived from various sources, depending on the supplier. The green chilies and the burrito mild sauce are vegan.

McDonald's also offers a lowfat apple bran muffin that contains sugar, egg whites, and whey. Ingredients of vegetable source in the muffin include mono- and diglycerides, natural flavors, and modified source starch. The cinnamon roll contains sugar and whole eggs, vegetable mono- and diglycerides, and vegetable-derived L-cysteine and natural flavors. The apple and cheese Danishes contain gelatin.

For dessert, McDonald's offers sundaes, apple pies, and cookies. The ice cream contains whole milk, sucrose, cream, non-fat milk solids, vegetable mono- and diglycerides, and synthetic vitamin A. The strawberry topping contains sugar and vegetable derived natural flavors. The hot fudge topping contains sugar, sweetened condensed skim milk, non-fat dry milk, vegetable lecithin, and animal derived polyglycerol esters of fatty acids. The hot caramel topping contains sweetened condensed whole milk, sucrose, and butter. McDonald's cones contain sugar and vegetable lecithin. McDonaldland cookies contain sugar and honey. The chocolate chip cookies contain sugar, butter, eggs, whey, and enzyme-modified butter oil from an animal source. The baked apple pie is made with sugar and lecithin and L-cysteine (an amino acid used as a dough conditioner). The latter two ingredients are derived from vegetable sources.

MIAMI SUBS: Miami Subs offer a veggie sub and a veggie pita. The sub roll contains dried egg yolks. The pita contains non-fat dry milk and enzymes of an unspecified source. A Swiss-American cheese blend or provolone cheese may be ordered on the sub or pita, but both menu items may be requested without cheese. The enzymes used to make the cheeses are of unspecified sources. The sandwiches also contain green peppers, black olives, mushrooms, tomatoes, onions, and a Romaine-iceberg lettuce mix.

Miami Subs also offers a large selection of salads. The garden salads consist of peppersini (hot pepper), a mix of iceberg and romaine lettuce, cucumbers, black olives, radishes, and green peppers. They have a Caesar salad, which contains Parmesan cheese made with an enzyme of an unspecified source. The Caesar dressing contains anchovies but the salad may be ordered without the dressing. The Greek salad contains feta cheese; no further information was given on the enzyme used to make this cheese. The Greek salad is served with the house dressing, a blend of vegetable oil and peppersini, and is vegan. Salad dressings that are offered at this restaurant chain include blue cheese, French, Thousand Island, fat-free honey mustard, and ranch dressings. Ingredient statements are listed on the salad dressing packets.

The French fries at Miami Subs are pre-blanched and cooked in all vegetable oil. The meat and seafood products are also cooked in this oil. The onion rings are coated in a batter that contains non-fat dry milk and whey.

The desserts at Miami Subs arrive pre-made at the restaurants. These include cheesecake and lime pie, both of which contain milk and eggs. No further information was available.

NATHAN'S: Their thick French fries, made from fresh potatoes at the restaurant, are cooked in unused corn oil. The potatoes are not treated or pre-cooked in any way.

OLIVE GARDEN: Olive Garden told us that they do not provide any information other than that stated in their menu and their brochures. Due to the large number of their food suppliers, many of which change, they cannot identify the sources of the ingredients used in their menu items. We were also informed that to suggest to readers that they call or ask at the restaurants about specific ingredients would be unproductive. Note also that menu variations may exist from restaurant to restaurant, even in a given city. Garden Fare® items, however, are standard in all Olive Garden restaurants.

PAPA JOHN'S: Papa John's uses only 100% mozzarella cheese on its pizza. A microbial rennet is used. The sauce contains no animal fats or flavors. It is made with canola and olive oils. The original dough is all vegan. The dough used to make the thin crust pizza contains olive oil and Parmesan cheese. Animal-derived rennet is used in the Parmesan cheese. It is possible to order a cheeseless pizza at Papa John's.

Papa John's also offers breadsticks and cheesesticks made from the original dough and mozzarella cheese, respectively. A side of pizza and garlic sauces is served with these items. The garlic sauce contains lactic acid, which has been produced by bacterial fermentation. Whey is a constituent of the bacterial growth medium. Papa John's informed us that according to food manufacturers' standards, the garlic sauce is "non-dairy." This implies that people with milk allergies would suffer no adverse effects from the sauce. The garlic sauce is normally spread on the cheesesticks, although they may be ordered without it. Vegan toppings include black olives, banana peppers, jalapeño peppers, pineapples, onions, green peppers, and mushrooms. Parmesan cheese is also offered; it has been made with animal-derived rennet.

PIZZA HUT: Pizza Hut's Thin 'n Crispy, Hand Tossed, and dessert crusts are vegan. The pan crust contains whey and enzymes, and the stuffed crust contains enzymes and mozzarella cheese (which is made with enzymes). Whey is an ingredient in the breadsticks, and enzymes and natural flavor are ingredients in their bread stick seasoning. All of the enzymes used in the cheeses at Pizza Hut are of unspecified sources.

The regular pizza sauce contains natural flavors of an unspecified source, whey, cheese solids (which is made with animal enzymes), buttermilk powder, nonfat milk solids, and MSG. The Cavatini, meatless, and bread stick sauces contains beef base, beef flavor, meat type flavor, natural flavor, and MSG. No further information was available on these ingredients. The Zesty pizza sauce contains chicken fat and two types of cheeses (made with enzymes). The sauce, which is served with the spaghetti marinara with meat, contains precooked sausage (composed of pork and beef), beef, chicken stock, chicken fat, and nonfat dry milk. All the pasta at Pizza Hut is vegan.

The sandwich cheese contains Swiss, American, and cheddar cheeses (all made with enzymes) and cream. The blue cheese dressing contains enzymes, egg yolk, and natural flavor. The ranch and buttermilk dressings contain cultured buttermilk, egg yolk, MSG, and natural flavor. The Romano dressing contains cheese, egg yolk, buttermilk powder, and MSG. The Italian dressing is vegan and contains MSG. The creamy cucumber dressing contains nonfat dry milk and natural sour cream flavor. The French dressing contains natural flavor. The Thousand Island dressing contains Worcestershire sauce (made with anchovies), natural flavorings, and egg yolk.

The dessert pizza cherry topping and icing are vegan. The dessert pizza blueberry and apple toppings contain natural flavors. The dessert pizza crumb topping contains mono- and diglycerides and natural flavor.

PIZZA PRO: Pizza Pro is mostly a carryout pizza chain. The mozzarella cheese used on the pizzas is vegetarian. The enzyme used to make the cheese is bioengineered chymax. The Parmesan cheese is made with an enzyme of unknown origin.

The crust and sauce are vegan. The cheesesticks, which contain mozzarella, Parmesan and Romano cheeses, are also made from pizza dough.

Some Pizza Pro restaurants serve salads. Some restaurants also serve ProSubs, which are composed of any type of cheese, lettuce, tomatoes, green peppers, black olives, and onions. The ProSub is made of a pre-made dough of which no further specifications were available.

Dessert items are not typically served at Pizza Pro restaurants although some may have cinnamon rolls on the menu.

PIZZERIA UNO CHICAGO BAR & GRILL: The thin crusts are vegan and the deep dish crust can be special ordered without cheese. The regular pizza sauce and the Uno pizza sauce are also vegan. The Uno sauce contains chunky tomatoes. Microbial rennet is used in the mozzarella, cheddar, and Muenster cheeses. The Romano cheese is also made with non-animal rennet.

Uno's serves a deep dish Veggie Pizza with cheese, mushrooms, onions, peppers, and tomato chunks. Other varieties include the Spinoccoli (topped with spinach and broccoli) and the Wild Mushroom deep-dish pizzas. No further information was available on the cheese blends used on these pizzas.

Uno's serves a Triple Mushroom thin crust pizza with mozzarella, Muenster, and asiago cheeses. The asiago cheese is made with an animal-derived enzyme. The Artipeggio pizza contains eggplant, marinated artichokes, red bell peppers, and a cheese blend. The Harvest pizza contains onions, mushrooms, peppers, broccoli, tomatoes, and special cheese. No further information was available on the special cheese. The Grilled Vegetable pizza contains a variety of grilled vegetables topped with mozzarella cheese. These vegetables, like all grilled vegetables at Uno's, are roasted on a grill used to prepare meat products, although not at the same time. The vegetables are brushed with olive oil and seasoned with herbs and spices. You may also order a cheeseless thin crust pizza, which has mushrooms, peppers, red onions, spinach, and broccoli.

Pizzeria Uno also serves pasta dishes. All pasta at Uno's is vegan. There is a vegan Grilled Vegetable Marinara served with ziti pasta. Freshly grated Parmesan cheese, made with animal-derived enzyme, is optional on this dish. The lasagna is made with meat sauce.

It is possible at Uno's to Pick-A-Pasta. You may choose the pasta (either ziti or fettuccine) and choose a sauce among the following: marinara (vegan), Alfredo, or creamy tomato Alfredo. No further information was available on the ingredients of the latter two sauces.

Also served at Pizzeria Uno is a Grilled Vegetable Roll-Up, which consists of grilled vegetables and a blend of cheeses served warm in a flour tortilla. This sandwich is served with French fries and ranch dressing on the side. No further information about the components of this entrée was available at this time.

Uno's also offers a number of salads including Pasta & Greens (marinated ziti pasta tossed with salad greens and served with Ike's dressing) and the House Salad (tomatoes, carrots, onions, peppers, cucumbers and croutons). Cheese is optional.

Appetizers include a veggie dip, garlic bread, nachos, and onion rings. Note that the cheese sticks are served with meat sauce and the pizza skins contain bacon. No further information concerning these appetizers was available at this time.

Uno's also serves soups. Cream of broccoli and tomato garden vegetable are among the offerings. No further information was available at this time.

POPEYE'S: The biscuits at Popeye's contain egg and buttermilk. The batter for the onion rings and the French fries contain eggs and dairy. These items are fried in a mix of beef tallow and vegetable (soybean) shortening. The corn on the cob is dipped into butter although a customer may request it without butter. The coleslaw contains mayonnaise. The apple pie at Popeye's is vegan.

RALLY'S: The French fries at Rally's have a batter, which contains beef tallow, whey, and MSG. They are fried in the same vegetable oil that is used to cook chicken. Onion rings, a new product at Rally's, contain whey and natural flavors of an unspecified source. They are also fried in vegetable oil that has been used to cook chicken.

It is possible to purchase a cheese sandwich with condiments or simply condiments on a bun at Rally's. The American cheese is made with an enzyme of unspecified source. The special sauce is vegan. It is a mix of ketchup, mustard, and dill relish. The seeded hamburger bun contains dry milk. The sausage bun is vegan.

Rally's offers a number of milkshakes, all of which contain milk, non-fat milk, whey, and cream. The banana and chocolate syrups used to make, respectively, the banana and chocolate shakes, contain natural flavors of an unspecified source. The red coloring in the strawberry shake is FD&C red No. 40.

Rally's serves several beverages including pink lemonade, kiwi-strawberry punch, and several teas.

RITA'S ITALIAN ICES: Rita's ices are vegan. There is no animal-derived color. They serve vanilla and chocolate custards, which contain dairy and egg whites.

Rita's also serves vegan pretzels. Butter, cheese, and icing may be optional toppings.

ROUND TABLE PIZZA: Round Table Pizza uses one type of dough for all of its pizzas and sandwiches. This dough contains non-fat dry milk. The standard cheese used on its pizzas, in the sandwiches, and at the salad bar, is a three-cheese mix composed of provolone, cheddar, and mozzarella cheeses. Of the three cheeses, only provolone is made with animal-derived rennet from a baby goat. Because the cheese is a mix, all cheese pizza at Round Table contains all three cheeses. However, it is possible to order a cheeseless pizza. Pizza toppings include artichoke hearts, black olives, garlic, mushrooms, pineapple tidbits, tomatoes, green peppers, red onions, jalapeño peppers, and zucchini. The sauce at Round Table is vegan.

There are several vegetarian pizzas on the menu at Round Table. All of them may be ordered on a thin or pan crust. The Gourmet Veggie™ Pizza is made with the creamy garlic sauce, which contains egg yolks and natural flavors of an unspecified source. It is topped with artichoke hearts, zucchini, spinach, mushrooms, Roma tomatoes, red and green onions, Italian herb seasoning, chopped garlic, and the three-cheese blend.

The Garden Pesto™ Pizza is made with pesto sauce, which contains Parmesan cheese. This cheese is made with an animal-derived enzyme. The pizza is topped with zucchini, artichoke hearts, Roma tomatoes, yellow and green onions, garlic, and the three-cheese blend.

Guinevere's Garden Delight™ Pizza is made with vegan tomato sauce and mushrooms, olives, Roma tomatoes, onions, green peppers, and the three-cheese blend.

Round Table also serves the Salute™ Veggie Pizza, which consists of the creamy garlic sauce, the three-cheese blend, artichoke hearts, zucchini, mushrooms, red onions, spinach, green onions, Roma tomatoes, green peppers, garlic, Italian herb seasoning, shredded Parmesan cheese, and roasted red peppers. An open butane-powered flame roasts the peppers.

There is one vegetarian sandwich, the Garden Vegetable sandwich, which is on the national menu. This sandwich is composed of artichoke hearts, black olives, red onions, and Roma tomatoes. It can be ordered without the standard cheese mix and the creamy garlic sauce. The sandwich bread dough is identical to the pizza dough, which contains non-fat dry milk.

Some Round Table restaurants may offer other varieties of sandwiches and some may serve salads. The selection of ingredients and dressings may vary widely from restaurant to restaurant.

Some Round Table Pizza restaurants with a salad bar may offer a lunch special consisting of a Gourmet Sandwich™ (such as the Garden Vegetable Sandwich) and your choice of Italian pasta salad, potato salad, macaroni salad, tortilla chips and salsa, or a green side salad. Some restaurants serve pre-made salads, which usually contain mayonnaise. This is true in the case of the potato and macaroni salads. The Italian pasta salad does not contain mayonnaise. It does contain Romano cheese made with an enzyme of unspecified source. Some Round Table restaurants may make the salads upon request according to the customer's specifications. You may always ask.

No further information was available on the ingredients in the tortilla chips and salsa. The customers create their own salads at the salad bar in restaurants that have this option.

Round Table Pizza also serves Garlic Parmesan Twists made

with the same dough used to make the pizzas. The Twist contains egg yolks and the Parmesan cheese is made with animal derived rennet. The Parmesan cheese, which is in canisters on the tables, is also made with animal derived rennet.

Desserts may be offered at some Round Table Pizza restaurants. The selection may vary. Ask the restaurant manager about ingredients.

SHAKEY'S PIZZA RESTAURANTS: There are two varieties of pizza crusts at Shakey's. Both are made with vegetable shortening and are vegan. The pizza sauce is also vegan. Mozzarella cheese made with a microbial enzyme is used on the pizzas. Shakey's offers a Garden Ranch Pizza, which is cheeseless. The crust is coated with garlic butter, which is actually vegetable margarine. Toppings on this pizza include tomatoes, green peppers, mushrooms, and roasted red peppers.

Shakey's also offers a wild mushroom pizza consisting of three varieties of mushrooms and the following four cheeses: asiago, Parmesan, fontina, and provolone. These cheeses are made with microbial enzymes. This pizza is made with specially prepared red onions, which give the pizza a distinct and robust flavor. You can also customize your own pizza at Shakey's by special ordering it.

Shakey's also offers a variety of vegan pastas. The marinara sauce served with many of the pasta entrées is vegan. The pomodoro sauce, composed of chunks of roma tomatoes, olive oil, basil, oregano, and garlic, is also vegan. The roasted red pepper sauce contains chicken stock and the bolognaise sauce is meat-based. The Alfredo sauce contains four cheeses. No further information on this sauce was available.

Shakey's offers a dish called Pasta Fresca. It consists of pasta and seven vegetables including yellow squash, zucchini, broccoli, carrots, and radishes. The vegetables are sautéed in olive oil on a skillet each time that this dish is ordered. The skillets are wiped down and dried between orders so there should not be any mixing of meat-based flavors from previously cooked dishes with the Pasta Fresca. The Pasta Fresca is served with a white wine sauce that contains white wine and dairy.

There are several pasta dishes containing meat on the menu at Shakey's. The pasta, vegetables, and meat are each cooked separately then added together late in the preparation. It would be possible to order one of these dishes without the meat.

Shakey's also offers mojo-potatoes, which are sliced, lightly floured potatoes. The flour contains an all-vegetable seasoning. This menu item is deep-fried in vegetable oil. The same oil is used to fry meat products.

There is an extensive salad bar at Shakey's restaurants. A three-bean salad is offered. Condiments may vary from location to location. You may be able to find alfalfa sprouts, sunflower seeds, and raisins. Salad dressings include Italian, French, Lite French, Ranch and Blue Cheese. No further information was available on these dressings. The individual restaurants purchase croutons so ingredients may vary. You may inquire about this or any condiment at any Shakey's if you want further specification on ingredients.

Ice cream, Jell-O (containing gelatin), and chocolate and vanilla puddings are offered for dessert. No further specifications were available on these menu items.

SKIPPER'S: Skipper's uses soybean oil for frying all their menu items. Their buns contain eggs. They offer a garden salad, which includes mixed greens and carrots. Other vegetarian foods include baked potatoes and coleslaw made with mayonnaise. The chocolate cake at Skipper's contains eggs and dairy.

SONIC DRIVE-IN RESTAURANTS: The French fries at Sonic Drive-In Restaurants have no beef product coating. The onion rings contain whey. Both of these menu items are cooked in vegetable oil. The meat products should be fried separately from the fries and onion rings although this policy may not be respected at all times.

This restaurant chain considered a veggie burger as a menu item, but company officials concluded that such an item was not economically feasible at this time. It is possible to order condiments on a bun at Sonic. However, local bakeries make the hamburger buns so be sure to ask the restaurant manager about ingredients. Condiments include ketchup, mustard, honey mustard, mayonnaise, lettuce, tomatoes, and pickles. The American cheese may contain either animal or vegetable derived enzymes.

Dessert items at Sonic include soft serve ice cream, which contains dairy. Sheet cake, which could also contain dairy as well as eggs, is served with ice cream.

STEAK ESCAPE: French fries at The Steak Escape are freshly cut and cooked in peanut oil. Only fries are cooked in this oil.

Vegetarians also have the choice of smashed potatoes, which consist of a baked potato served with sautéed vegetables. The

grill used to sauté these and all vegetables is also used to prepare meat although the grill surface is scraped clean between
orders.

It is also possible at this restaurant chain to request a
meatless sandwich. The multi-grain and white rolls contain no
eggs or dairy. Sautéed vegetables may be served on the
sandwich. Swiss and provolone cheeses are offered; both are
made with animal derived rennet. Condiments include mayonnaise and yellow, brown, and German mustards.

Salads may be ordered without cheese. Among the salad
dressings that are available are Kraft Ranch and Italian dressings.

Dessert items at The Steak Escape include chocolate chip,
white chocolate Macadamia nut, peanut butter, and oatmeal
raisin cookies. All of the varieties contain eggs and dairy.

SUBWAY: Subway is the only restaurant chain of its type which
has achieved the right to use the "Five a Day for Better Health"
logo of the Produce for Better Health Foundation which works in
conjunction with the National Cancer Institute. Subway's menu
items, several of which are low in fat, and 100% of which contain
vegetables, meet the rather strict standards of this organization.

A Veggie Delight™ Salad is on the national menu at Subway. It
consists of lettuce, tomatoes, onions, pickles, green peppers,
and olives. Dressings include Creamy Italian, Fat-Free Italian,
French, Fat-Free French, Thousand Island, Ranch, and Fat-Free
Ranch dressings.   Ingredient statements appear on the
individually labeled packages in the restaurants. Subway also
offers a vegetable/olive oil blend and vinegar that can be used as
a dressing. Red wine vinegar is used in this dressing.

American cheese is an optional item on this salad. The
cheese may be made with either animal (pig or calf) or microbial
rennet, or chemically engineered chymosin, an enzyme. Other
varieties of cheeses, such as provolone, lowfat American, Swiss,
or mozzarella, may be available at certain Subway restaurants.
The source of the enzyme could vary in these varieties as well.

The Veggie Delight™ Salad may be ordered on a sub roll. Subway offers a wheat sub roll, which contains honey and powdered honey. The Italian white roll is vegan. Subway also serves other sandwiches on a deli-style bun, which contains whole egg product.

All of Subway's bread products contain vegetable-based mono- and diglycerides. Subway also reports that the L-cysteine used in its bread dough is synthetically derived or derived from wheat protein.

It is also possible at Subway to order a cheese sub. A wheat or white sub roll is typically used for this sandwich. Optional condiments, which are free of charge, include oil, vinegar, mayonnaise or light mayonnaise, and mustard. This sandwich, as are all of Subway's sandwiches and salads, is built according to the customer's specifications. It is possible to request extra vegetable toppings as well, free of charge.

Subway restaurants have the choice of offering a few other menu items besides those on the national menu. Among them is a meatless burger. The most popular brands are Wholesome & Hearty's Gardenburger® and Morningstar Farms' Veggie-Max®. Both of these items contain egg whites and dairy products (cheese or caseinate). Vegan Boca Burgers or White Wave soy turkey subs may be offered at certain Subway restaurants in some areas. The "turkey" in the soy turkey sub is vegan but the soy cheese used on it contains casein. If you are interested in seeing a veggie burger in your area, contact your local Subway restaurant.

Subway also serves cookies. All varieties are made with vegetable shortening and eggs. Whey solids are in the chocolate chunk cookies and may be present in some of the other varieties as well. A concerned customer may inquire about the ingredients at the restaurant.

Certain Subway restaurants serve breakfast items and/or soups. Selections and ingredients may vary. You may inquire at the particular restaurant about ingredients in a locally offered menu item.

Subway is testing Fruizle™ Smoothie (a non-dairy, fat-free, fruit-based drink) and lowfat frozen swirled yogurt in certain markets. The smoothie is made with frozen or canned fruit in its own natural juice and fruit syrups and juices. It contains unrefined cane sugar and other sugars of an unknown source. There are twelve blend-ins. Some are in powdered form and others are veggie-encapsulated ingredients such as wheat grass or wheat germ powder, which may be added to the Fruizle™. Subway's lowfat gelatin-free frozen swirl yogurt comes in vanilla and chocolate flavors.

TACO BELL: The Veggie Fajita Wrap™ at Taco Bell consists of roasted fresh peppers and onions, seasoned rice, tomatoes, a blend of cheddar, pepper jack, and mozzarella cheeses and fajita sauce in a soft flour tortilla. It can be ordered without the sauce (which contains chicken and clam extract) and rice (which contains chicken flavoring). The chicken flavoring is currently in the process of being added to all rice served at all Taco Bell restaurants. The rice also contains non-fat dry milk.

The Veggie Fajita Wrap Supreme™ is a Veggie Fajita Wrap™ served with sour cream. The sour cream at Taco Bell contains gelatin. The vegetables in both of the Veggie Fajita Wraps have been roasted on an open gas flame then frozen. When they arrive at Taco Bell restaurants they are reheated in a clean container and kept warm on a steam table. The soft flour tortilla does not contain milk. The cheeses at Taco Bell may contain enzymes from any source.

Taco Bell's 7-Layer Burrito consists of beans, seasoned rice, lettuce, tomatoes, sour cream, guacamole, and a blend of four cheeses: shredded Monterey Jack, American, mozzarella, and cheddar cheeses. The guacamole does not contain sour cream.

The corn tortillas (hard tacos) at Taco Bell are vegan. The wheat tortillas (soft tacos) and the tortillas used for burritos are also vegan. The pinto beans, which arrive pre-cooked and mashed at Taco Bell restaurants and are simply rewarmed but not refried before being served, are vegan.

Taco Bell also serves a bean burrito consisting of a soft flour tortilla filled with beans, cheddar cheese, red sauce and onions. The red sauce is vegan.

Other sauces that are available at Taco Bell include the mild and hot taco sauces, salsa, green sauce, and Pico de Gallo. All of these sauces are vegan. The newest sauce is the Fire Sauce, which contains natural flavors of an unspecified source. The hot and mild taco sauces and Fire sauces are available in packets at no extra charge. It is possible to substitute green sauce for red sauce in any menu item at no extra charge. There may be an additional charge for the other sauces.

The tortilla chips and tacos arrive pre-made at the restaurants. The taco salad, tostada, and pizza shells are fried at the restaurants. Corn oil is used in all frying processes. There are no meat products fried in this oil.

The tortilla chips are served with nacho cheese sauce. This sauce contains cheddar cheese, whey, non-fat dry milk, and the following ingredients of unspecified source: natural flavors and mono- and diglycerides. The tostada consists of a corn tortilla topped with pinto beans, red sauce, lettuce, and cheddar cheese. The Mexican Pizza and Taco Salad, both made of a soft flour tortilla, contain meat. It may be possible at some Taco Bell restaurants to purchase these menu items without the meat. You may always ask.

Ranch dressing is served with the taco salad at some Taco Bell restaurants. Vendors may vary so check the packet or inquire about ingredient information at the particular Taco Bell. The ranch dressing most likely contains eggs and dairy and possibly other ingredients of concern to some vegetarians.

Taco Bell also offers a kid's meal consisting of a bean burrito, nacho chips, cheese sauce (described above), and a drink.

The Cinnamon Twists are made of wheat, corn, and rice flours and all vegetable seasoning. The Twists are fried at the restaurants where the pizza and tostada shells are fried. No meat products are fried along with these vegetarian items. The Border Ice products are also vegan.

There are some Taco Bell restaurants which serve breakfast items. The country gravy contains dairy products and is served with the Country Breakfast Burrito, which may be purchased without the sausage at some Taco Bell restaurants. The Breakfast Quesadilla consists of a soft flour tortilla filled with scrambled eggs, melted cheddar and pepper jack cheeses, and red sauce. The precooked eggs contain butter and natural flavors of an unspecified source. They arrive at the restaurants in plastic bags and are re-heated in hot water while in the bags. These are not cooked further on a grill along with meat products.

Taco Bell no longer serves its Light menu. They no longer offer fat-free sour cream or fat-free cheddar cheese. Menu offerings may vary regionally. Franchised Taco Bell restaurants and Taco Bell Express Restaurants may not serve all corporate-approved items

TACO CABANA: Taco Cabana could not identify the source of the enzymes used in their cheeses. Their suppliers change according to the market price. In all markets except the Denver area restaurants, the refried beans contain bacon fat and the rice contains chicken stock. In the Denver area restaurants, vegetarian refried beans are used and the rice seasoning is all vegetarian. Taco Cabana reported that only in the Denver region were vegetarian alternatives justified due to consumer interest.

Spinach enchiladas are also on the menu in the Denver area, although sometimes they or similar items may be offered elsewhere in the nation. The spinach enchilada contains cheese, and the sauce contains sour cream and milk. Except for the cheese, the Caesar salad offered in the southwest restaurants is vegan. Their black bean tacos and burritos contain no bacon fat.

TACO JOHN'S INTERNATIONAL: Vegetarian items at Taco John's include bean burritos made with beans cooked in canola oil. No lard or tropical oils are used in any products or food preparation.

There is no animal rennet in the cheeses at Taco John's. The burritos and enchiladas are made with a wheat tortilla. Two companies supply the wheat tortillas. Both brands contain whey and one brand contains mono- and diglycerides. The bean burrito comes with cheese, but a customer may order the item without cheese. The Corporate Communications and Public Relations Manager at Taco John's International, who is a vegetarian, suggested that tomatoes might be added to the cheeseless bean burrito to make a great tasting meal. In fact, she said that any item on the menu may be made vegetarian by substituting beans for meat. The taco and fajita salads contain shells, which are fried in the same oil used to cook the meat products. The guacamole contains modified food starch but is otherwise vegan.

Both the nachos and Potato Ole's® are fried in the same oil as the meat products. Taco John's uses three brands of corn tortillas, (all of which are vegan), to make their nachos. In some restaurants the sour cream may contain gelatin. It is always best to ask the restaurant manager. The Potato Ole's® contain natural flavorings that do not contain any animal products.

TACO TICO: This restaurant chain serves several items that are veggie-friendly. The tortilla chips and Tico de Gallo sauce, composed of tomatoes, onions, garlic and cilantro, are vegan. They serve a Fresh Mex Wrap, which consists of Mexican rice, black beans, cheddar cheese, and the following vegetables cooked in vegetable oil: mushrooms, carrots, and black olives blended with the Tico de Gallo sauce. The mixture is wrapped in a soft flour tortilla, which is vegan. It is possible to purchase this wrap without the cheese. No further information was available on the Mexican rice or on the cheese.

Taco Tico offers vegetarian burritos. The tortilla filled with refried beans and topped with the Tico de Gallo sauce is vegan. Vegetarians may opt for the same burrito with cheddar cheese. Lettuce and tomatoes are optional.

Deep-fried corn tostadas are available. All-vegetable oil is used to fry the shells and no meat products are fried in the same vat. The tostada is served with vegan refried beans, lettuce, tomatoes, cheese, and sauce of choice. There are vegan hot, mild, and green chili sauces from which to choose. This menu item may be purchased without the cheese.

Gelatin-free guacamole is served at some restaurants, and will be added to the chain-wide standard menu in the near future. No information was available on the sour cream.

For dessert, Taco Tico serves Cinnamon Crustos, which are deep-fried flour tortillas covered with cinnamon and sugar. This item is not fried along with meat products. The choco taco is chocolate-covered ice cream in a crispy corn taco shell.

TCBY: All the soft-serve frozen yogurt contains the following ingredients: milk, non-fat dry milk, cane sugar, cream, and natural flavor of unspecified nature. The hand-dipped ice cream and yogurt contain vegetable mono- and diglycerides. The sorbet contains sugar and mono- and diglycerides of an unspecified nature. No information was available on TCBY's toppings.

T.G.I. Friday's: T.G.I. Friday's vegetarian items include Cheddar Cheese Nachos, Friday's Gardenburger, Spinach & Feta Pizzadilla, Veggie Wrapper, Broken Noodles, and Fettuccine Alfredo, all of which contain dairy products. Their baked goods also contain dairy, but contain no animal shortening. Rennet from an unspecified source is used in Friday's cheeses. Friday's Mushrooms are another vegetarian option, but they are cooked in the same (vegetable) shortening as meat/seafood products. Vegan items include Friday's House Salad and the Fresh Vegetable Medley, when ordered with a plain baked potato instead of the brown rice pilaf. The brown rice pilaf has chicken base in it. All of their soups contain animal-derived natural flavors. The refried beans contain bacon grease. The Vegetable Baguette and the Garden Cobb are no longer on the menu. T.G.I. Friday's will gladly prepare menu items on request in order to accommodate vegetarians or others with special dietary needs.

TONY ROMA'S, A PLACE FOR RIBS: This restaurant chain serves an onion ring loaf, which has been coated with a milk-containing egg wash. It is fried in all-vegetable oil that is used to cook meat products. The French fries are also cooked in this oil.

Tony Roma's serves a baked potato, which may be topped with sour cream, butter, cheddar cheese, or chives. No further information was available on the cheese.

There is a side dinner salad on the menu, which consists of lettuce, tomatoes, onions, and croutons. Dressings include honey mustard, Italian (which contains Parmesan cheese), blue cheese (which contains dairy), ranch (which contains buttermilk), and Thousand Island. The dressing for the Caesar salad contains eggs and dairy but no anchovies. No further information was available on the croutons or the dressings.

WENDY'S: Wendy's receives high marks for its attempts to educate its customers about the ingredients in its menu offerings. Their February 1997 Nutrition Guide brochure is among the most detailed of all the restaurant chains. For instance, their source of mono- and diglycerides (vegetable) is listed each time this ingredient appears. The brochure also indicates in parentheses the function (e.g., preservative, flavor enhancer, etc.) of many ingredients so the consumer understands the reason for having that ingredient in the food.

There are two corrections to the February 1997 brochure, which Wendy's asked us to mention. First, a typographical error was made in the description of the Garden Veggie Pita. Contrary to the information given, there is no Parmesan cheese in this pita sandwich. (However, the pita bread does contain skim milk, L-cysteine, an amino acid of an unspecified source, and enzymes of an unspecified source.)

Secondly, by August 1997 Wendy's should have changed the formula for the Reduced Fat/Reduced Calorie Garden Ranch Sauce. Due to a customer's request, gelatin will no longer be an ingredient in this sauce.

Wendy's explained to us that since the summer of 1996 when

chicken nuggets were introduced, the possibility exists that their French fries and hash browns (the latter only in the few Wendy's which serve breakfast) could be fried in the same oil used to cook meat and seafood products. Normally, fries and hash browns are cooked in different vats. However, when the demand for fries is high, it may be necessary to cook them in a vat normally reserved for meat or seafood products. Wendy's suggests that if a person is concerned about this, he should request that the fries be cooked in a vat reserved only for French fries. Wendy's would be happy to comply with this request. The French fries at Wendy's contain no natural flavors that are animal-derived. The fries are pre-blanched in partially hydrogenated soybean oil.

All of the enzymes used in Wendy's cheeses are derived from vegetable or microbial sources. There is no MSG in any of the foods served at Wendy's. Nor is there hydrolyzed vegetable protein, a vegan ingredient which is composed of 40-45% salt and 9-12% monosodium glutamate. Note, however, that one of Wendy's suppliers of sour cream does use gelatin derived from pork in its formulation. The concerned customer can ask the restaurant manager to check the ingredient label in order to find out which type of gelatin is used at a particular Wendy's restaurant.

Wendy's offers a selection of salads and dressings, both to carry out and to eat-in. The deluxe garden salad and the side salad are both vegetarian, but do list 'imitation cheese' as an ingredient, which according to the product ingredient information does not contain enzymes.

Vegan dressings include the French and Reduced Fat/Reduced Calorie Italian dressings. Their Fat-Free French dressing contains honey. The Hidden Valley Ranch dressing contains eggs, and the Reduced Fat/Reduced Calorie Hidden Valley Ranch and Blue Cheese dressings contain eggs and dairy. The Italian Caesar dressing contain anchovy paste and Worcestershire sauce (which contains anchovies), and the Reduced Fat/Reduced Calorie Caesar Vinaigrette contains anchovies.

Wendy's also offers a vegetarian sandwich, which is a choice of toppings on a bun without meat. Their Kaiser and sandwich buns contain whey. Wendy's did perform a "concept test" of a grain-based burger in some shopping malls. The results showed that such an item was not popular enough to merit test marketing at this time. If you would like Wendy's to offer a veggie burger, contact their consumer relations department at (614) 764-6800.

WESTERN SIZZLIN: The vegetarian and vegan items at the hot and cold food bars may vary greatly from one Western Sizzlin to the next. Recipes for certain items may likewise vary. It is always best to inquire at the particular restaurant when you are in doubt.

Some of the thirty to forty items that you may typically find at the cold food bars include potato salad and coleslaw, garbanzo beans, and fresh vegetables. There are plenty of ingredients for garden salads. Dressings include the following: ranch (contains buttermilk), blue cheese (contains blue cheese, buttermilk, and mayonnaise), Thousand Island (contains egg yolks), and oil and vinegar.

There are many prepared vegetables at the hot food bars. The mashed potatoes contain milk and the green beans contain pork flavoring. Soup may be available. The vegetable soup contains beef broth.

It is possible to order condiments on a bun. Most Western Sizzlin restaurants have their own bakeries and most of their bread products contain dairy. Inquire at the bakery about the ingredients in any bread product.

It is also possible to order a cheese sandwich. The types of cheeses commonly available at this restaurant chain include mozzarella, American, and cheddar, although offerings may vary from restaurant to restaurant. Because of the variation in suppliers of the cheeses, no further specification about the enzyme used to make the cheeses could be given.

WESTERN STEER FAMILY RESTAURANTS: Western Steer offers a large buffet, which includes several hot and cold menu items. Among the cooked vegetables, the green beans, broccoli, and turnip greens are prepared in bacon stock. The steamed squash and carrots are prepared in all-vegetable stock. The mashed potatoes contain milk and butter.

The French fries at this restaurant chain are all vegetable. They are fried separately in vegetable oil.

At the cold bar of the buffet is a wide selection of mayonnaise-based salads. There are a large number of raw vegetables at the salad bar. There may be a three-bean salad, pickled beets, soy nuts, alfalfa sprouts, sunflower seeds, and raisins. Ken's salad dressings are used. Varieties include ranch, tomato vinaigrette (vegan), Caesar (no anchovies), Italian, cucumber and honey Dijon. No further specifications were available.

For dessert, this restaurant chain offers chocolate cookies, which contains eggs.

Two years ago during a short period, Western Steer test-marketed a veggie burger. Due to low consumer demand, it was not added to the menu.

WHATABURGER: The French fries at Whataburger are all vegetable. They are fried in a vat of vegetable shortening apart from the meat/seafood products. The onion rings contain whey, non-fat milk, and egg whites. They are cooked in the same way as the French fries.

The wheat buns contain honey, lactose (milk sugar), and mono- and diglycerides of an unspecified source. The white buns contain skim milk and mono- and diglycerides of an unspecified source.

Whataburger offers a garden salad composed of iceberg lettuce, tomatoes, carrots, purple cabbage, green bell pepper, and cucumbers. The club crackers and croutons contain whey. The croutons also contain dehydrated Romano cheese, non-fat milk, and the following ingredients of unspecified source: disodium inosinate and disodium guanylate.

The low-fat ranch dressing contains dehydrated buttermilk and sour cream, egg yolks, and natural flavors of an unspecified source. The ranch dressing contains egg yolk and buttermilk solids. It also contains unspecified natural flavorings. The Thousand Island dressing contains egg yolk and unspecified natural flavorings. The low-fat vinaigrette dressing is vegan.

Breakfast entrees at Whataburger include the potato and egg taquito, which consists of a flour tortilla, scrambled eggs, and hash browns. The tortilla contains dry milk and the scrambled eggs contain low-fat milk. The all-vegetable hash browns contain unspecified natural flavors and are fried in vegetable shortening in a vat used for vegetable products only.

Whataburger also serves an egg sandwich. The eggs are prepared on the same grill with meat products. Their egg sandwich is served on a white bun (described above). Processed American cheese, made with an enzyme of unspecified source, is a part of this sandwich although the sandwich may be ordered without the cheese. A biscuit and egg sandwich is served on a buttermilk biscuit, which contains buttermilk and mono- and diglycerides of an unspecified source. All-vegetable margarine is used. Processed American cheese and scrambled eggs (described above) are a part of this sandwich.

Whataburger also serves Texas toast, which is white bread prepared in the bun toaster with all-vegetable bun oil. Cheese may be requested on the toast.

The buttermilk pancakes contain buttermilk, whey, egg yolk, and egg white. The pancake syrup is vegan.

The cinnamon rolls contain whey, non-fat milk, and the following ingredients of an unspecified nature: mono- and diglycerides and enzymes. The blueberry muffins contain non-fat skim milk and eggs. The all-vegetable apple turnovers contain unspecified natural flavorings. The apple turnovers are fried in vegetable shortening in a vat for vegetable products only.

For dessert, Whataburger serves chocolate chunk, oatmeal raisin, peanut butter, and white chocolate chunk macadamia nut cookies, all of which contain butter and eggs. The milk shakes contain milk, cream, non-fat milk solids, whey, cane sugar, and mono- and diglycerides of an unspecified source. The chocolate syrup used in the chocolate shakes contains vegetable mono- and diglycerides and polysorbate 80, an emulsifier of unspecified source. The malt-flavored syrup used in the milk shakes contains an antifoam emulsion of an unspecified source. The strawberry syrup used in the strawberry shakes is vegan. The following shakes may be ordered at Whataburger: vanilla, vanilla-malt, chocolate, chocolate-malt, strawberry, and strawberry-malt.

Whataburger reports that all of their menu items can be made to the customer's specification. It is possible to order cheese and condiments on a bun at Whataburger.

The Vegetarian Resource Group (VRG) has been providing information on vegetarian food offered at restaurant chains for over fifteen years. Special thanks to Jeanne-Marie Bartas for doing this update. Readers should let us know if they hear of any new vegetarian items being offered at restaurant chains. Write to The VRG at PO Box 1463, Baltimore, MD 21203. Our e-mail address is <vrg@vrg.org> and our web site is at <www.vrg.org>.

RECIPES

The toughest barriers to quick and easy vegetarian cooking are the habits we have developed throughout our lifetime. Once you break that mental resistance, ideas for meals will come to you naturally, and meal preparation will become routine and go much faster.

This section has some ideas to get you started. You may want to adjust the amount of spices to your taste. Eliminate salt and soy sauce or tamari and use low sodium tomato sauce and tomato paste if you are on a low sodium diet. If you are on a lowfat diet, when a recipe calls for oil for sautéing vegetables, use slightly more water or vegetable broth instead of the oil.

Recipes were analyzed using Nutritionist IV and manufacturer's information. Optional ingredients were omitted. If ingredient choices were listed (i.e. green or red cabbage), the first ingredient was used in analysis. If a range of servings was specified (i.e. 4-6), the lowest number of servings was used for analysis.

Breakfast Ideas

BROILED GRAPEFRUIT
(Serves 4)

2 large grapefruits, sliced in half, seeds removed
2 Tablespoons maple syrup
1/2 teaspoon cinnamon

Loosen grapefruit sections with a knife. Place grapefruit halves fruit side up on a baking pan and spread 1/2 Tablespoon maple syrup on each half. Sprinkle 1/8 teaspoon cinnamon on each grapefruit half and place under a broiler for 7 minutes. Serve warm.

Total calories per serving: 98
Fat: <1 gram   Total Fat as % of Daily Value: <1%
Protein: 2 grams   Iron: 1 mg   Carbohydrate: 24 grams
Calcium: 81 mg   Dietary fiber: 11 grams

APPLESAUCE
(Serves 6)

6 apples, diced finely
1 Tablespoon cinnamon
1 teaspoon nutmeg
2 oranges, peeled and sliced
Water

Put about 1/3-inch of water in a large pot. Add all the ingredients and cook over medium heat until the apples are soft, stirring occasionally. For variety you can add 1/4 cup raisins.

Total calories per serving: 103
Fat: 2 grams   Total Fat as % of Daily Value: 2%
Protein: 1 gram   Iron: <1 mg   Carbohydrate: 26 grams
Calcium: 27 mg   Dietary fiber: 4 grams

OATMEAL/APPLES/RAISINS AND CINNAMON
(Serves 4)

1 cup rolled oats
3 cups water
2 apples, chopped
1/2 cup raisins
1 teaspoon cinnamon

Heat the above ingredients together in a pot over medium heat for about 5 minutes until oats are cooked. Stir occasionally to prevent sticking.

Total calories per serving: 173
Fat: 2 grams   Total Fat as % of Daily Value: 3%
Protein: 4 grams   Iron: 1 mg   Carbohydrate: 38 grams
Calcium: 24 mg   Dietary fiber: 3 grams

CORNMEAL MUSH
(Serves 2)

1/2 cup quick cooking cornmeal
1-1/2 cups water
1/2 cup chopped fresh fruit (blueberries, bananas, straw-
    berries, etc.)

Cook corn meal in water according to directions on the box, adding chopped fruit just before serving.

Total calories per serving: 163
Fat: 1 gram   Total Fat as % of Daily Value: 2%
Protein: 3 grams   Iron: 2 mg   Carbohydrate: 36 grams
Calcium: 5 mg   Dietary fiber: 3 grams

CINNAMON/SLICED APPLE TOAST
(Serves 6)

6 slices whole wheat bread or English muffins
2-3 apples, thinly sliced
1 Tablespoon brown sugar (optional)
1 Tablespoon margarine
1/2 teaspoon cinnamon

Toast bread. Place several slices of apple, dots of margarine, sprinkle of brown sugar, and a dash of cinnamon on toast or muffin. Place under a broiler until the margarine melts.

Total calories per serving: 114
Fat: 3 grams   Total Fat as % of Daily Value: 5%
Protein: 3 grams   Iron: 1 mg   Carbohydrate: 20 grams
Calcium: 24 mg   Dietary fiber: 1 gram

CORNBREAD AND BLUEBERRIES
(Serves 6)

8-ounce box vegan cornbread mix (Beware: some mixes contain lard!)
1 cup blueberries

Preheat oven to 350 degrees. Add blueberries to batter prepared from a cornbread mix. Pour into lightly oiled 9-inch square cake pan. Bake until done at 350 degrees (approximately 15 minutes).

Total calories per serving: 161
Fat: 4 grams   Total Fat as % of Daily Value: 6%
Protein: 3 grams   Iron: 1 mg   Carbohydrate: 30 grams
Calcium: 1 mg   Dietary fiber: 1 gram

EGGLESS BANANA PANCAKES
(Serves 2)

1/2 cup rolled oats
1/2 cup whole wheat pastry flour or unbleached white flour
1/2 cup cornmeal (white or yellow)
1 Tablespoon baking powder
1-1/2 cups water
2 large ripe bananas, sliced or mashed
2 teaspoons oil

Mix all the ingredients together in a bowl. Use about 1/4 cup of batter per pancake, poured into lightly oiled preheated frying pan. Fry over low heat on one side until light brown, then flip over and fry on the other side until done.

Variations: Add chopped apples, raisins, or blueberries to the batter before frying.

Total calories per serving: 482
Fat: 8 grams   Total Fat as % of Daily Value: 12%
Protein: 12 grams   Iron: 4 mg   Carbohydrate: 97 grams
Calcium: 306 mg   Dietary fiber: 9 grams

EGGLESS FRENCH TOAST
(Serves 3-4)

3 ripe bananas
1 cup soy or rice milk
2 Tablespoons molasses or maple syrup
1/4 teaspoon cinnamon
7 slices whole wheat bread
2 teaspoons oil

Mash bananas in a bowl. Add soy or rice milk, molasses or maple syrup, and cinnamon. Stir well.

Soak bread in above mixture. Fry in lightly oiled frying pan on both sides over medium heat until lightly brown.

Total calories per serving: 380
Fat: 9 grams   Total Fat as % of Daily Value: 14%
Protein: 10 grams   Iron: 4 mg   Carbohydrate: 70 grams
Calcium: 121 mg   Dietary fiber: 2 grams

HASH BROWN POTATOES
(Serves 4)

2 teaspoons oil
4 large white potatoes, cleaned and thinly sliced
1 large onion, chopped
1/2 teaspoon garlic powder
1/4 teaspoon paprika
Salt and pepper to taste

Heat oil in a frying pan over a medium-high heat. Add potatoes
and onion. Add seasonings and stir-fry until potatoes are soft
(about 15 minutes).

Total calories per serving: 307
Fat: 3 grams   Total Fat as % of Daily Value: 5%
Protein: 6 grams   Iron: 4 mg   Carbohydrate: 66 grams
Calcium: 31 mg   Dietary fiber: 7 grams

Beverages

HOT APPLE CIDER
(Serves 8)

1/2 gallon apple cider
1 lemon, sliced thinly
1-1/2 teaspoons cinnamon
1/4 teaspoon nutmeg

Heat all the above ingredients in a large pot over medium heat, stirring occasionally, until heated through. Serve warm in mugs.

Total calories per serving: 127
Fat: <1 gram   Total Fat as % of Daily Value: <1%
Protein: <1 gram   Iron: 1 mg   Carbohydrate: 36 grams
Calcium: 23 mg   Dietary fiber: <1 gram

BLENDED FRUIT DRINK
(Serves 4)

3 ripe bananas, sliced
6 strawberries
4 cups chilled orange juice

Blend all the ingredients above in a blender and serve.

Variations: Use different fruit juices and or other fruits such as peaches and apples.

Total calories per serving: 195
Fat: 1 gram   Total Fat as % of Daily Value: 2%
Protein: 3 grams   Iron: 1 mg   Carbohydrate: 48 grams
Calcium: 29 mg   Dietary fiber: 2 grams

QUICK CASHEW MILK
(Serves 4)

1 cup raw cashews
3 cups water

Blend the cashews and water in a blender for 5 minutes and refrigerate. Use as a beverage or in recipes calling for milk. Shake well before serving.

Total calories per serving: 196
Fat: 16 grams   Total Fat as % of Daily Value: 25%
Protein: 5 grams   Iron: 2 mg   Carbohydrate: 11 grams
Calcium: 16 mg   Dietary fiber: 2 grams

EASY ALMOND NUT MILK
(Serves 2)

1/2 cup almonds
1-1/2 cups boiling water

Blend almonds and boiling water in a blender for about 3 minutes at a high speed. Strain through muslin or cheesecloth. (The remaining pulp can be used in burgers or vegetable/nut loaves.) Shake milk well before serving.

Total calories per serving: 172
Fat: 15 grams   Total Fat as % of Daily Value: 24%
Protein: 8 grams   Iron: 2 mg   Carbohydrate: 6 grams
Calcium: 114 mg   Dietary fiber: 3 grams

MILK SHAKE
(Serves 3)

3 cups chilled nut milk (see above recipes)
6 Tablespoons cocoa or carob powder
2/3 cup shredded coconut
Sweetener to taste (maple syrup, etc.)

Blend above ingredients together in a blender at a high speed for 2 minutes. Serve immediately.

Total calories per serving (using cashew milk): 373
Fat: 24 grams   Total Fat as % of Daily Value: 37%
Protein: 8 grams   Iron: 4 mg   Carbohydrate: 35 grams
Calcium: 32 mg   Dietary fiber: 5 grams

SPARKLING SELTZER
(Serves 1)

8 ounces seltzer (salt-free)
2 Tablespoons frozen juice concentrate (orange, grapefruit, lemon, grape, etc.)

Pour chilled seltzer into a glass. Add frozen juice concentrate. Stir well, and enjoy!

Variation: Add 1/2 cup juice instead of frozen concentrate to 1/2 cup seltzer.

Total calories per serving (using orange juice concentrate): 56
Fat: <1 gram   Total Fat as % of Daily Value: <1%
Protein: 1 gram   Iron: <1 mg   Carbohydrate: 14 grams
Calcium: 19 mg   Dietary fiber: <1 gram

Salads and Dressings

COLESLAW
(Serves 4)

1/2 medium head green cabbage, shredded
4 carrots, grated
1/2 cup lemon juice
1/2 cup eggless mayonnaise (found in natural foods stores)

Mix all the ingredients together in a large bowl. Chill and toss before serving.

Variations: Add grated apples, crushed pineapple, raisins, and/ or toasted sunflower seeds.

Total calories per serving: 129
Fat: 6 grams   Total Fat as % of Daily Value: 9%
Protein: 2 grams   Iron: 1 mg   Carbohydrate: 16 grams
Calcium: 65 mg   Dietary fiber: 3 grams

A HEFTY SALAD
(Serves 4)

1 stalk celery, diced
1 large carrot, grated
1 clove garlic, minced (optional)
1/2 cup toasted sunflower or pumpkin seeds
2 Tablespoons eggless mayonnaise or dressing of choice
Salt and pepper to taste
1/2 pound lettuce or raw spinach leaves

Mix ingredients (except lettuce or spinach leaves) well in a large bowl and serve on 1/2 pound lettuce or raw spinach leaves.

Total calories per serving (including lettuce): 139
Fat: 11 grams   Total Fat as % of Daily Value: 17%
Protein: 5 grams   Iron: 2 mg   Carbohydrate: 8 grams
Calcium: 42 mg   Dietary fiber: 3 grams

STUFFED TOMATO SALAD
(Serves 5)

5 large ripe tomatoes
8-ounce can chickpeas (or about 1 cup precooked chick-
** peas)**
1 stalk celery, chopped (optional)
Salt and pepper to taste

Scoop out tomatoes, saving pulp to use as a sauce. Fill tomatoes with chickpeas and celery. Season with salt and pepper. Garnish with sauce and lettuce or sprouts.

Total calories per serving: 80
Fat: 2 grams   Total Fat as % of Daily Value: 3%
Protein: 3 grams   Iron: 1 mg   Carbohydrate: 15 grams
Calcium: 24 mg   Dietary fiber: 5 grams

CUCUMBER SALAD
(Serves 6)

3 cucumbers, sliced
1/2 cup white vinegar
1 small onion, minced
Pepper to taste

Mix all the ingredients together in a bowl. Serve immediately; however, the salad tastes better if allowed to sit in the refrigerator for a day or two. Store in a jar.

Total calories per serving: 26
Fat: <1 gram   Total Fat as % of Daily Value: <1%
Protein: 1 gram   Iron: 1 mg   Carbohydrate: 6 grams
Calcium: 25 mg   Dietary fiber: <1 gram

BEET SALAD
(Serves 4)

2 large beets, grated
1/2 medium head cabbage, shredded
3 carrots, grated
Handful of raisins
1 apple, diced
1/4 cup lemon juice
1/4 cup oil
1/4 cup water

Toss all the ingredients together in a large bowl and mix well.

Variations: Use raw sweet potato instead of beets. Add sunflower seeds, crushed pineapple, or other fruit.

Total calories per serving: 232
Fat: 14 grams   Total Fat as % of Daily Value: 21%
Protein: 3 grams   Iron: 1 mg   Carbohydrate: 27 grams
Calcium: 71 mg   Dietary fiber: 4 grams

SUMMER FRUIT SALAD
(Serves 12)

Large fresh pineapple
6 large pieces other fruit (i.e. apples, peaches, plums, etc.)
3 Tablespoons shredded coconut

Stand pineapple upright and cut it in half vertically. Carve out pineapple into bite size pieces. Cut up additional fruit into small pieces. Mix all the fruit together and pour back into pineapple shell. Sprinkle with shredded coconut and serve chilled.

Total calories per serving (using apples, peaches, and plums): 65
Fat: 1 gram   Total Fat as % of Daily Value: 2%
Protein: 1 gram   Iron: <1 mg   Carbohydrate: 15 grams
Calcium: 7 mg   Dietary fiber: 2 grams

POTATO SALAD AND OLIVES
(Serves 4)

4 large white potatoes, peeled and cubed into small pieces
Water
10-ounce box frozen mixed vegetables
1 small onion, chopped finely
1/3 cup black olives, drained and sliced
1 teaspoon celery seed
Salt and pepper to taste
1/2 cup eggless mayonnaise

Cover potatoes with water in a large pot and cook until tender over medium heat. Drain potatoes. At the same time, cook mixed vegetables in a separate pot until tender. Drain vegetables. Mix the ingredients together in a large bowl. Season and add mayonnaise according to your taste.

Variations: Instead of frozen vegetables, add raw vegetables such as finely chopped celery and/or carrots. Add finely chopped parsley. You may also want to use canned pre-cooked Irish potatoes to save more time.

Total calories per serving: 348
Fat: 12 grams   Total Fat as % of Daily Value: 18%
Protein: 9 grams   Iron: 4 mg   Carbohydrate: 55 grams
Calcium: 80 mg   Dietary fiber: 8 grams

MACARONI SALAD
(Serves 6)

3 cups pre-cooked macaroni
2 stalks celery, diced
1 carrot, diced
1 cup peas (frozen or fresh), cooked
1 small onion, finely chopped
Eggless mayonnaise to taste
Salt and pepper to taste

Mix all the ingredients together in a large bowl.

Variations: Add sliced pickles, other vegetables, or olives.

Total calories per serving (using ½ cup mayonnaise): 152
Fat: 4 grams   Total Fat as % of Daily Value: 6%
Protein: 4 grams   Iron: 1 mg   Carbohydrate: 6 grams
Calcium: 9 mg   Dietary fiber: 2 grams

TOMATO SALAD
(Serves 4)

4 tomatoes, cut into 1/2-inch wedges
2 Tablespoons oil
1/4 cup water
1 teaspoon lemon juice
2 cloves garlic, minced
Oregano and salt to taste

Mix all the ingredients together in a bowl and serve.

Total calories per serving: 89
Fat: 7 grams   Total Fat as % of Daily Value: 11%
Protein: 1 gram   Iron: 1 mg   Carbohydrate: 6 grams
Calcium: 9 mg   Dietary fiber: 2 grams

CRANBERRY SALAD
(Serves 12)

12 ounces fresh or frozen cranberries
1/2 cup orange juice or apple juice
1 cup raisins
1 cup shredded coconut
2 stalks celery, chopped finely
1 apple, chopped finely
1/4 cup chopped walnuts (optional)

Blend cranberries, juice, and raisins together in a blender. Pour into a large bowl and add coconut, celery, apple, and walnuts if desired. Toss well before serving.

Total calories per serving: 102
Fat: 3 grams   Total Fat as % of Daily Value: 5%
Protein: 1 gram   Iron: 1 mg   Carbohydrate: 20 grams
Calcium: 14 mg   Dietary fiber: 2 grams

SWEET RAINBOW DELIGHT
(Serves 6)

3 apples, grated
3 carrots, grated
1/3 cup shredded coconut
1/2 cup raisins

Toss all the ingredients together in a bowl and serve.

Variation: Add chopped dates instead of raisins.

Total calories per serving: 116
Fat: 2 grams   Total Fat as % of Daily Value: 3%
Protein: 1 gram   Iron: 1 mg   Carbohydrate: 26 grams
Calcium: 21 mg   Dietary fiber: 3 grams

RAW VEGETABLE PLATTER
(Serves 12)

Chop up into bite-size pieces 3 to 4 pounds of vegetables including: celery, carrots, broccoli, tomatoes, squash, and mushrooms. Arrange on a large platter. Serve with your favorite dips and spreads or the dressings below.

Nutritional breakdown will vary depending upon vegetables and dressings selected.

SWEET FRENCH DRESSING
(Makes 2 cups)

1 cup oil
2 oranges, peeled and seeds taken out
2 Tablespoons lemon juice
1 Tablespoon white vinegar
1 teaspoon paprika
1 teaspoon salt
Slice of onion, minced

Blend all the ingredients together in a blender for 3 minutes and serve over your favorite salad or raw vegetables.

Total calories per 2 Tablespoon serving: 129
Fat: 14 grams   Total Fat as % of Daily Value: 22%
Protein: <1 gram   Iron: <1 mg   Carbohydrate: 2 grams
Calcium: 7 mg   Dietary fiber: <1 gram

LEMON/APPLE/GARLIC DRESSING
(Makes 3 cups)

1 cup white vinegar
1-1/2 cups water
2 Tablespoons lemon juice
2 cloves garlic, minced
1/4 teaspoon pepper
1/4 teaspoon salt
1 apple — peeled, cored and chopped

Blend all the ingredients together in a blender for 3 minutes. You can use this lowfat dressing instead of mayonnaise in potato, macaroni, and other salads.

Total calories per 2 Tablespoon serving: 5
Fat: <1 gram   Total Fat as % of Daily Value: <1%
Protein: <1 gram   Iron: <1 mg   Carbohydrate: 2 grams
Calcium: 2 mg   Dietary fiber: <1 gram

RED BEET DRESSING
(Makes 2 cups)

1 beet, peeled and chopped
1 cup orange juice
1/2 cup oil
1 clove garlic, minced
Salt and pepper to taste

Blend all the ingredients together in a blender for 3 minutes.

Total calories per 2 Tablespoon serving: 69
Fat: 7 grams   Total Fat as % of Daily Value: 11%
Protein: <1 gram   Iron: <1 mg   Carbohydrate: 2 grams
Calcium: 2 mg   Dietary fiber: <1 gram

Soups

VEGETABLE RICE SOUP
(Serves 6-8)

1 cup white rice
6 cups water
1/2 cup parsley, chopped
10-ounce box frozen mixed vegetables
1 medium onion, chopped
Pepper and salt to taste

Cook all the ingredients in a large pot over medium heat until rice is tender (about 30 minutes).

Total calories per serving: 153
Fat: <1 gram   Total Fat as % of Daily Value: <1%
Protein: 4 grams   Iron: 2 mg   Carbohydrate: 34 grams
Calcium: 25 mg   Dietary fiber: 2 grams

FRESH TOMATO SOUP
(Serves 4)

1 large onion, chopped
5 small ripe tomatoes, chopped
1-1/2 cups water
1 teaspoon dried parsley flakes or 2 teaspoons fresh parsley, minced
Dash of pepper and salt

Combine ingredients in a large pot. Cook over medium heat for 15 minutes. Cool a few minutes; then blend in a blender, reheat, and serve warm.

Total calories per serving: 36
Fat: <1 gram   Total Fat as % of Daily Value: <1%
Protein: 1 gram   Iron: 1 mg   Carbohydrate: 8 grams
Calcium: 12 mg   Dietary fiber: 2 grams

CREAMED CARROT SOUP
(Serves 6)

1 pound carrots, chopped
1 large onion, chopped
1-1/2 Tablespoons oil
6 cups water
1/2 teaspoon salt
1/3 cup fresh parsley, finely chopped

Sauté the chopped onions and carrots in oil for 5 minutes in a large pot. Add water, salt, and parsley. Bring to a boil. Reduce heat, cover, and simmer for 20 more minutes. Puree mixture in a blender and reheat.

Total calories per serving: 72
Fat: 4 grams   Total Fat as % of Daily Value: 6%
Protein: 1 gram   Iron: 1 mg   Carbohydrate: 10 grams
Calcium: 29 mg   Dietary fiber: 2 grams

CREAM OF BROCCOLI SOUP
(Serves 8)

1 pound broccoli, chopped
1/2 pound mushrooms, chopped
1 small onion, chopped
1 teaspoon tarragon
3 cups soy and/or rice milk
Salt and pepper to taste

Steam vegetables and onion together for 10 minutes. Blend half of the steamed vegetables in a blender or food processor along with 1-1/2 cups soy and/or rice milk. Pour into a large pot. Blend remaining steamed vegetables and soy and/or rice milk. Add to pot. Season with tarragon, salt, and pepper, and reheat for 5 minutes over medium heat. Add water if you prefer thinner soup. Serve warm.

Total calories per serving: 86
Fat: 3 grams   Total Fat as % of Daily Value: 5%
Protein: 6 grams   Iron: 1 mg   Carbohydrate: 10 grams
Calcium: 60 mg   Dietary fiber: 3 grams

CREAMED ZUCCHINI/POTATO SOUP
(Serves 6)

1 small onion, chopped
3 Tablespoons oil
3 or 4 medium zucchini, chopped
2 large white potatoes, scrubbed and cut into small cubes
6 cups water
1/2 cup rolled oats
1/2 teaspoon salt
2 Tablespoons fresh parsley, finely chopped

Sauté onion in oil in a large pot for 2 minutes. Add chopped zucchini and cubed potatoes. Sauté for 5 minutes longer. Add water, oats, and seasoning. Simmer for 15 minutes. Puree mixture in a blender, reheat, and serve warm.

Total calories per serving: 168
Fat: 8 grams   Total Fat as % of Daily Value: 12%
Protein: 4 grams   Iron: 2 mg   Carbohydrate: 23 grams
Calcium: 35 mg   Dietary fiber: 3 grams

Lunch Ideas

MOCK "TUNA" SALAD
(Serves 3)

1 cup chickpeas (canned or pre-cooked and drained)
1 stalk celery
1/2 small onion, finely chopped
3 Tablespoons eggless mayonnaise
Salt and pepper to taste

Mash the chickpeas in a small bowl. Add remaining ingredients and mix well. Spread on whole grain bread as a sandwich or serve on a bed of lettuce.

Total calories per serving: 122
Fat: 5 grams   Total Fat as % of Daily Value: 8%
Protein: 4 grams   Iron: 1 mg   Carbohydrate: 17 grams
Calcium: 35 mg   Dietary fiber: 5 grams

SPINACH/MUSHROOM SANDWICH
(Serves 6)

10-ounce box frozen spinach
1 cup mushrooms, sliced finely
1 pint sour cream (look for non-dairy sour cream found in
    natural food stores and kosher supermarkets)
6 thick slices whole grain bread or English muffins

Cook spinach per instructions on box and drain well. Place cooked spinach and sliced mushrooms on the bread. Cover with sour cream. Place in toaster oven under low heat until hot. Serve warm.

Total calories per serving: 184
Fat: 9 grams   Total Fat as % of Daily Value: 14%
Protein: 7 grams   Iron: 2 mg   Carbohydrate: 22 grams
Calcium: 354 mg   Dietary fiber: 4 grams

QUICK PIZZA
(Serves 6)

3 English muffins or 6 slices whole wheat bread
1 cup tomato sauce
6 slices vegan cheese
Italian seasoning to taste
1/2 cup chopped vegetables (i.e. sliced onion, chopped
green peppers, sliced mushrooms, and/or sliced olives)

Toast the English muffin or bread.   Spoon sauce over top of
bread.   Lay slices of cheese on top.   Season to taste.   Put on
optional toppings and place pizza in a toaster oven until the
cheese melts (approximately 5-10 minutes).   Serve warm.

Total calories per serving: 128
Fat: 3 grams   Total Fat as % of Daily Value: 5%
Protein: 4 grams   Iron: 1 mg   Carbohydrate: 20 grams
Calcium: 244 mg   Dietary fiber: 1 gram

POTATO PANCAKES
(Serves 6)

3 cups cooked white potatoes, mashed
1 small onion, chopped
Salt and pepper to taste
1/4 cup fresh parsley, finely chopped (optional)
2 Tablespoons oil

Mix the mashed potatoes, onion, and seasonings together. Heat oil in a large frying pan. Pour pancakes onto heated pan and fry on each side until light brown (about 8 minutes per side). Serve warm alone or with applesauce.

Total calories per serving: 113
Fat: 5 grams   Total Fat as % of Daily Value: 8%
Protein: 2 grams   Iron: <1 mg   Carbohydrate: 17 grams
Calcium: 6 mg   Dietary fiber: 1 gram

CORN FRITTERS
(Serves 6)

2 cups corn kernels (fresh, frozen, or canned and drained)
1 cup flour
1-1/2 Tablespoons corn starch
1-1/4 cups water
1 Tablespoon oil

Mix all the ingredients (except oil) in a medium-size bowl. Pour batter into a lightly oiled frying pan over medium heat and fry for 3-5 minutes. Turn fritters over and continue frying for 3 minutes longer. Serve warm.

Variations: Instead of corn use other chopped vegetables.

Total calories per serving: 157
Fat: 3 grams   Total Fat as % of Daily Value: 5%
Protein: 4 grams   Iron: 1 mg   Carbohydrate: 18 grams
Calcium: 3 mg   Dietary fiber: 2 grams

COUSCOUS/SQUASH BURGERS
(Makes 12 — serve 2 burgers per person)

3 cups cooked couscous (about 3/4 of 10-ounce box)
1-1/2 pounds grated zucchini and/or yellow squash
1/2 small onion, finely chopped
1/2 cup unbleached white flour
2-1/2 teaspoons marjoram
Salt and pepper to taste
1 Tablespoon oil

Mix all the ingredients (except oil) together. Using wet hands, form 12 flat burgers. Fry for 10 minutes on each side in a lightly oiled frying pan over medium-high heat. Serve warm alone or on whole wheat buns for sandwiches.

Total calories per serving: 176
Fat: 3 grams   Total Fat as % of Daily Value: 5%
Protein: 6 grams   Iron: 1 mg   Carbohydrate: 33 grams
Calcium: 27 mg   Dietary fiber: 6 grams

RICE BURGERS
(Makes 6 burgers)

2 cups rice, cooked (leftover cooked rice is great)
1/2 cup bread crumbs
1 cup mixed vegetables (i.e. celery, carrots, squash,
    broccoli), finely chopped
Salt and pepper to taste
1/3 cup oil

Mix rice, bread crumbs, vegetables, and seasonings together. Using wet hands, form 6 flat burgers. Fry for 8-10 minutes on each side in a lightly oiled frying pan over medium-high heat. Serve warm alone or on whole wheat buns with lettuce for sandwiches.

Variations: Instead of cooked rice, use cooked barley. Also, add a small onion, finely chopped.

Total calories per burger (using celery, carrots, squash, and broccoli): 223
Fat: 13 grams   Total Fat as % of Daily Value: 20%
Protein: 3 grams   Iron: 1 mg   Carbohydrate: 25 grams
Calcium: 18 mg   Dietary fiber: 1 gram

LENTIL BURGERS
(Makes 6)

1 cup lentils, pre-cooked in 2-1/2 cups water and drained
1 small onion, finely chopped
1/2 cup wheat germ
1/2 teaspoon garlic powder
Salt and pepper to taste
1 Tablespoon oil

Mix all the ingredients together. Using wet hands, form 6 patties. Fry for 10 minutes on each side in a lightly oiled frying pan over medium heat. Serve warm alone or on a roll with lettuce and tomato.

Total calories per burger: 147
Fat: 4 grams   Total Fat as % of Daily Value: 6%
Protein: 10 grams   Iron: 3 mg   Carbohydrate: 21 grams
Calcium: 21 mg   Dietary fiber: 4 grams

Side Dishes

CAULIFLOWER AU GRATIN
(Serves 4)

10-ounce box frozen cauliflower
1-1/2 cups bread crumbs
2 teaspoons oil
4 slices vegan cheese, cut into strips
Salt and pepper to taste

Cook cauliflower according to directions on the box and drain. Preheat oven to 350 degrees. Roll cooked cauliflower in bread crumbs and place in oiled baking dish. Add strips of cheese and seasoning. Bake at 350 degrees until cheese melts.

Total calories per serving: 225
Fat: 7 grams   Total Fat as % of Daily Value: 11%
Protein: 8 grams   Iron: 2 mg   Carbohydrate: 34 grams
Calcium: 245 mg   Dietary fiber: 3 grams

SCALLOPED CORN AND TOMATOES
(Serves 6)

2 Teaspoons oil
4 large tomatoes, sliced thickly
15-ounce can corn kernels, drained or 10-ounce box frozen
    corn kernels
1 cup bread crumbs
2 Tablespoons margarine

Preheat oven to 350 degrees. Spread oil in an approximately 8-inch x 2-inch tall round baking dish. Place tomatoes on the bottom and mix in the corn. Top with bread crumbs and dot with margarine. Bake at 350 degrees about 20 minutes or until crumbs are toasted. Serve warm.

Total calories per serving: 201
Fat: 7 grams   Total Fat as % of Daily Value: 11%
Protein: 6 grams   Iron: 1 mg   Carbohydrate: 18 grams
Calcium: 27 mg   Dietary fiber: 4 grams

LEFTOVER POTATO DISH
(Serves 6)

2 Tablespoons oil
2 cups leftover baked or boiled potatoes, sliced
1 large onion, chopped
1 cup leftover cooked vegetables
Paprika, garlic powder, salt, and pepper to taste

Heat oil in a large frying pan over medium-high heat. Fry potatoes and onions for 5 minutes. Add vegetables and seasonings
and continue heating for 5 more minutes. Serve warm.

Total calories per serving (using broccoli and carrots): 114
Fat: 5 grams   Total Fat as % of Daily Value: 8%
Protein: 2 grams   Iron: 1 mg   Carbohydrate: 17 grams
Calcium: 21 mg   Dietary fiber: 2 grams

GREEN BEANS WITH HERB SAUCE
(Serves 4)

10-ounce box frozen French-style green beans
1/2 small onion, finely chopped
2 Tablespoons vegan margarine
1 Tablespoon fresh parsley, finely chopped
1/4 teaspoon thyme
1-1/2 Tablespoons lemon juice
Paprika, salt, and pepper to taste

Cook green beans per directions on box and drain. Place cooked green beans in a serving dish. Sauté onion in margarine in a medium-size frying pan over medium heat for 3 minutes. Add remaining ingredients and mix well. Once heated pour over cooked green beans and serve.

Total calories per serving: 72
Fat: 6 grams   Total Fat as % of Daily Value: 9%
Protein: 1 gram   Iron: 1 mg   Carbohydrate: 6 grams
Calcium: 38 mg   Dietary fiber: 1 gram

SAUTÉED MUSHROOMS
(Serves 4)

2 Tablespoons vegan margarine or oil
1 pound mushrooms, cleaned and chopped
1 large onion, finely chopped
Garlic powder, salt, and pepper to taste

Heat margarine or oil in a large frying pan over medium-high heat. Sauté mushrooms and onion for 5 minutes. Season to taste and cook over low heat for 3 minutes longer or until mushrooms are tender. Serve warm.

Total calories per serving: 89
Fat: 6 grams   Total Fat as % of Daily Value: 9%
Protein: 3 grams   Iron: 1 mg   Carbohydrate: 8 grams
Calcium: 14 mg   Dietary fiber: 2 grams

CABBAGE DISH
(Serves 6)

1 Tablespoon oil
1 medium-size head green cabbage, shredded
1/2 cup toasted sesame seeds
6 slices vegan cheese

Sauté cabbage and sesame seeds in oil in a large frying pan over medium-high heat until cabbage is tender. Add strips of cheese and cook over low heat until cheese melts. Serve warm.

Variation: Use lettuce, spinach, or bok choy instead of cabbage.

Total calories per serving: 162
Fat: 10 grams   Total Fat as % of Daily Value: 15%
Protein: 5 grams   Iron: 2 mg   Carbohydrate: 13 grams
Calcium: 362 mg   Dietary fiber: 4 grams

SPANISH RICE
(Serves 3)

1 medium onion, finely chopped
1 large green pepper — cored, seeds removed, and chopped
2 teaspoons oil
1/4 cup water or vegetable broth
1-1/2 cups rice, pre-cooked (leftovers are good)
3 large ripe tomatoes, cubed
8-ounce can tomato sauce
Pepper, cumin, and chili powder to taste

Sauté onion and green pepper in oil in a large frying pan over medium heat for 3 minutes. Add remaining ingredients and cook 10 more minutes, stirring occasionally to prevent sticking. Serve.

Total calories per serving: 222
Fat: 4 grams   Total Fat as % of Daily Value: 6%
Protein: 5 grams   Iron: 3 mg   Carbohydrate: 43 grams
Calcium: 29 mg   Dietary fiber: 4 grams

STUFFED MUSHROOMS
(Serves 4)

12 large mushrooms
1/2 cup vegetable broth or water
1 small ripe avocado
1 small ripe tomato, finely chopped
Pinch of cayenne pepper and garlic powder
Salt to taste

Remove stems from mushrooms. Sauté mushroom caps in broth or water for a few minutes until soft. Remove from heat and allow to cool. Mash avocado in a small bowl. Add tomato and seasonings. Mix well. Stuff mushrooms with avocado mixture and serve.

Total calories per serving: 90
Fat: 7 grams   Total Fat as % of Daily Value: 11%
Protein: 4 grams   Iron: 1 mg   Carbohydrate: 7 grams
Calcium: 8 mg   Dietary fiber: 1 gram

FRIED ZUCCHINI AND SAUCE
(Serves 4)

1 Tablespoon oil
2 pounds zucchini, sliced lengthwise 1/2-inch thick
Italian seasoning, salt, and pepper to taste
8-ounce can tomato sauce

Fry zucchini slices in oil in a large covered frying pan with seasonings for 5 minutes over medium heat. Flip zucchini over, cover with tomato sauce, and continue cooking over low heat for 10 minutes. Serve warm.

Total calories per serving: 78
Fat: 4 grams   Total Fat as % of Daily Value: 6%
Protein: 3 grams   Iron: 2 mg   Carbohydrate: 16 grams
Calcium: 41 mg   Dietary fiber: 3 grams

SWEET AND SOUR CABBAGE
(Serves 6)

1 small head cabbage (red and/or green), shredded
1 large onion, chopped
2 Tablespoons oil
1/2 cup raisins
1 large apple, grated
1/2 cup water
2 Tablespoons unbleached white flour
2 Tablespoons vinegar
1 Tablespoon brown sugar or other granulated sweetener
2 teaspoons salt
1/2 cup water

Sauté onions and cabbage in oil in a large frying pan over a medium heat for 8 minutes. Add raisins, apple, and 1/2 cup water. Cook 5 minutes longer. In a small jar, shake up flour, vinegar, sugar, salt, and 1/2 cup water. Add to frying pan and cook another 8 minutes. Serve warm.

Variation: Use crushed pineapple instead of grated apple.

Total calories per serving: 142
Fat: 5 grams   Total Fat as % of Daily Value: 8%
Protein: 2 grams   Iron: 1 mg   Carbohydrate: 25 grams
Calcium: 57 mg   Dietary fiber: 3 grams

PASTA DISH
(Serves 4)

3 Tablespoons vegan margarine
1/4 teaspoon each oregano, basil, salt, and black pepper
1/2 teaspoon garlic powder
1/4 cup fresh parsley, finely chopped (optional)
1 pound pasta, cooked and drained
3 Tablespoons vegan Parmesan cheese or nutritional yeast

Melt margarine in a large pot and add seasonings. Stir in cooked pasta, sprinkle on cheese or yeast, and serve warm.

Total calories per serving: 509
Fat: 10 grams   Total Fat as % of Daily Value: 15%
Protein: 17 grams   Iron: 4 mg   Carbohydrate: 86 grams
Calcium: 69 mg   Dietary fiber: 0 grams

Main Dishes

RIGATONI COMBINATION
(Serves 6)

1/3 pound rigatoni shells, macaroni, or other pasta
1 large onion, chopped
1 clove garlic, minced
1/2 large green pepper, chopped
2 teaspoons olive oil
8-ounce can tomato sauce
16-ounce can kidney beans, drained
1 teaspoon soy sauce or tamari
1/2 teaspoon chili powder
Pepper and salt to taste

Cook pasta according to package directions. Sauté onion, garlic, and green pepper in oil for 5 minutes in a large pot. Stir in tomato sauce, kidney beans, soy sauce or tamari, and seasonings. Simmer several minutes to heat through. Drain pasta when done cooking and stir into sauce. Serve as is or add hot sauce if desired.

Total calories per serving: 181
Fat: 2 grams   Total Fat as % of Daily Value: 3%
Protein: 8 grams   Iron: 3 mg   Carbohydrate: 33 grams
Calcium: 36 mg   Dietary fiber: 6 grams

TOMATO/EGGPLANT BAKE
(Serves 4)

1 Tablespoon oil
1 small eggplant, peeled and cut into small pieces
15-ounce can stewed tomatoes
1 onion, finely chopped
1 large green pepper, finely chopped

Preheat oven to 350 degrees. Place eggplant, stewed tomatoes, onion, and green pepper in a large oiled baking dish. Bake at 350 degrees until done (approximately 20 minutes). Serve warm.

Total calories per serving: 100
Fat: 4 grams   Total Fat as % of Daily Value: 6%
Protein: 2 grams   Iron: 1 mg   Carbohydrate: 16 grams
Calcium: 54 mg   Dietary fiber: 3 grams

BROCCOLI/KASHA BAKE
(Serves 6)

10-ounce box frozen broccoli
1-1/2 cups kasha, uncooked
4 slices vegan cheese
1 Tablespoon oil

Preheat oven to 350 degrees. Cook broccoli per package directions and drain. Cook kasha in water until done. Mash broccoli and mix well with kasha. Place in a medium-size oiled baking dish. Lay slices of cheese on top. Bake at 350 degrees until cheese melts. Serve warm.

Total calories per serving: 205
Fat: 5 grams   Total Fat as % of Daily Value: 8%
Protein: 7 grams   Iron: 1 mg   Carbohydrate: 36 grams
Calcium: 156 mg   Dietary fiber: 5 grams

VEGETARIAN STEW
(Serves 4)

1/2 cup corn kernels (fresh, frozen, or canned)
1/2 cup lima beans (fresh, frozen, or canned)
1/2 cup potatoes (pre-cooked or canned)
1/2 cup stewed tomatoes
1 medium onion, chopped
1 teaspoon oregano
1/4 cup fresh parsley, finely chopped
Salt and pepper to taste

Mix above ingredients in a large pot. Cook over low heat until heated through (about 12 minutes). Serve alone or over rice.

Total calories per serving: 87
Fat: <1 gram   Total Fat as % of Daily Value: <1%
Protein: 3 grams   Iron: 1 mg   Carbohydrate: 15 grams
Calcium: 28 mg   Dietary fiber: 3 grams

LEFTOVER STEW
(Serves 4)

1 Tablespoon oil
1 small onion, chopped
1 green pepper, chopped
3 stalks celery, chopped
1 cup crushed tomatoes
2 cups leftovers (pre-cooked beans, seeds or nuts, raisins,
    grains, vegetables, olives, etc.)
Salt, pepper, and Italian seasoning to taste

Sauté onion, green pepper, and celery in oil in a large pot. Add tomatoes, leftovers, and seasonings. Cook over medium heat 10-15 minutes and serve warm.

Total calories per serving (using kidney beans and rice): 171
Fat: 4 grams   Total Fat as % of Daily Value: 6%
Protein: 6 grams   Iron: 2 mg   Carbohydrate: 29 grams
Calcium: 52 mg   Dietary fiber: 5 grams

MACARONI/CABBAGE DISH
(Serves 4)

1-1/2 cups macaroni
6 cups water
1/2 medium cabbage, shredded
1 medium onion, chopped
1 large green pepper, chopped
1/2 cup vegetable broth
Salt and pepper to taste

Cook macaroni in boiling water until tender and drain. Meanwhile, sauté cabbage, onion, and green pepper in vegetable broth in a large pot over medium heat for 10 minutes. Add cooked macaroni and seasoning and heat 5 minutes longer. Serve warm.

Total calories per serving: 187
Fat: 1 gram   Total Fat as % of Daily Value: 2%
Protein: 7 grams   Iron: 2 mg   Carbohydrate: 39 grams
Calcium: 59 mg   Dietary fiber: 3 grams

VEGETABLE POT PIE
(Serves 8)

Crust: This is a quick crust that can be used in many different recipes. (In a rush use a store-bought pie crust.)

2 cups whole wheat pastry flour or unbleached white flour
1/2 teaspoon salt
1/2 cup vegan margarine
1/2 cup water

Mix flour and salt in bowl. Work in margarine with fingers. Add water, stirring as little as possible to form a ball. Divide into 2 equal balls and roll out to 1/8-inch thickness. Prick pie shells and bake in pie pans at 400 degrees for 10 minutes.

Vegetable Filling:

1/2 cup vegetable broth
1 cup onions, chopped
1 cup celery, chopped
1/2 cup carrots, chopped
1-1/4 cups peas (fresh or frozen)

Sauté above ingredients in broth until onions are soft. In a separate bowl mix the following:

1/4 cup oil
1/2 cup unbleached white flour
1-2/3 cups water
1/2 teaspoon garlic powder
1 teaspoon salt
1/3 teaspoon pepper

Preheat oven to 350 degrees. Add above mixture to sautéed vegetables. Pour into one pie shell and cover with the other pie shell. Bake at 350 degrees until crust is brown (approximately 15-20 minutes).

Total calories per serving: 320
Fat: 18 grams   Total Fat as % of Daily Value: 28%
Protein: 7 grams   Iron: 2 mg   Carbohydrate: 34 grams
Calcium: 33 mg   Dietary fiber: 6 grams

VEGETARIAN CHILI
(Serves 6)

1 Tablespoon oil
1 large onion, chopped
3 cloves garlic, minced
1 large green pepper, chopped
3 cups water
1 cup kidney beans (pre-cooked or canned)
4 large ripe tomatoes, chopped
1 cup corn kernels (fresh, frozen, or canned)
1 teaspoon salt
1 teaspoon chili powder
Pepper to taste

In a large pot sauté the onion, garlic, and green pepper in oil over medium heat until the onion is soft. Add water, kidney beans, tomatoes, corn, salt, chili powder, and pepper. Cook 25 minutes longer.

Variations: Add hot peppers, other vegetables such as carrots and celery, or add 2/3 cup bulgur (cracked wheat). Pinto beans may be used instead of kidney beans.

Total calories per serving: 118
Fat: 3 grams   Total Fat as % of Daily Value: 5%
Protein: 5 grams   Iron: 1 mg   Carbohydrate: 15 grams
Calcium: 28 mg   Dietary fiber: 5 grams

RATATOUILLE
(Serves 4)

1/2 cup vegetable broth
3 large ripe tomatoes, chopped
1 large zucchini, chopped
1 small eggplant, cubed
1 large green pepper, chopped
1 large onion, chopped
2-3 cloves garlic, minced

In a large frying pan sauté the tomatoes, zucchini, eggplant, peppers, onions, and garlic in broth over low heat for 15 minutes. Serve warm over a bed of rice or slice of bread.

Total calories per serving: 81
Fat: 1 gram   Total Fat as % of Daily Value: 2%
Protein: 3 grams   Iron: 1 mg   Carbohydrate: 18 grams
Calcium: 36 mg   Dietary fiber: 3 grams

SPAGHETTI AND VEGETABLE SAUCE
(Serves 4)

Cook 1 pound of spaghetti and drain.

Sauce:

2 teaspoons oil
1 large onion, chopped
2 cloves garlic, minced
15-ounce can tomato sauce
6-ounce can tomato paste
1 small zucchini, sliced
2 carrots, chopped
1 cup mushrooms, sliced
Italian seasoning, salt, and pepper to taste

Sauté onion and garlic in oil in a large pot over low heat for 5 minutes. Add sauce, paste, vegetables, and seasoning. Cook 20 minutes longer. Serve warm over cooked pasta.

Total calories per serving: 529
Fat: 5 grams   Total Fat as % of Daily Value: 8%
Protein: 18 grams   Iron: 8 mg   Carbohydrate: 104 grams
Calcium: 65 mg   Dietary fiber: 7 grams

FRIED EGGPLANT
(Serves 4)

1 large eggplant
1/4 cup oil
1 cup bread crumbs (or crushed corn flakes or matzo meal)
1 medium onion, chopped
3 cloves garlic, minced

Slice eggplant. Add one Tablespoon oil to bread crumbs. Dip eggplant slices into crumbs. Fry eggplant, onion, and garlic in remaining oil over medium heat for 10 minutes.

Variations: Top with vegan Parmesan cheese, tomato sauce, and/or Italian seasoning.

Total calories per serving: 269
Fat: 15 grams   Total Fat as % of Daily Value: 23%
Protein: 5 grams   Iron: 1 mg   Carbohydrate: 30 grams
Calcium: 50 mg   Dietary fiber: 1 gram

LENTIL STEW
(Serves 6)

1 cup lentils
1 cup macaroni or other pasta
15-ounce can tomato sauce
6-ounce can tomato paste
1 large onion, chopped
1 teaspoon Italian seasoning
1 teaspoon garlic powder
4 cups water

Cook all ingredients in a large pot over medium heat until tender (approximately 20 minutes). Serve warm.

Total calories per serving: 203
Fat: 1 gram   Total Fat as % of Daily Value: 2%
Protein: 11 grams   Iron: 5 mg   Carbohydrate: 39 grams
Calcium: 40 mg   Dietary fiber: 7 grams

ZUCCHINI BAKE
(Serves 4)

2 large zucchini, sliced
4 slices vegan cheese
15-ounce can tomato sauce
Salt and pepper to taste

Preheat oven to 325 degrees. Place alternating layers of zucchini, cheese, and tomato sauce in a medium-size baking dish. Season to taste. Bake at 325 degrees for 20-25 minutes. Serve hot.

Total calories per serving: 95
Fat: 3 grams   Total Fat as % of Daily Value: 5%
Protein: 4 grams   Iron: 2 mg   Carbohydrate: 14 grams
Calcium: 222 mg   Dietary fiber: 3 grams

Soy Dishes

Although tofu and tempeh may not be familiar products to you, we have chosen to include them because they are convenient soy food products. Tofu can be found in most supermarkets today. If you've eaten in Chinese restaurants, you probably have eaten some tofu. It would have been called soybean curd. Tofu can be used to make dips and soups, desserts such as strawberry tofu cheesecake, and side or main dishes such as curried tofu or fried tofu, which has a texture similar to fried chicken. Unfortunately, tempeh is still only found in some supermarkets and is more likely to be found in a natural foods store. It is a fermented soy product and has a meaty texture. Tempeh can be prepared in a variety of ways.

TOFU MAYONNAISE DIP
(Serves 8)

16-ounces tofu, drained (soft or silken tofu is best)
1/2 teaspoon prepared mustard
2 teaspoons lemon juice
1 Tablespoon olive or vegetable oil
3 Tablespoons water
1 large clove garlic, minced
1/4 teaspoon salt
1 Tablespoon soy sauce or tamari
1/2 teaspoon Louisiana-style hot sauce (optional)
1/2 teaspoon rice or maple syrup (optional)

Blend all the ingredients in a food processor until very smooth. Use as a dressing for potato, macaroni, or rice salads; or use as a dip for raw vegetables. If you want a simple mayonnaise, omit the last four ingredients.

Total calories per serving: 48
Fat: 3 grams   Total Fat as % of Daily Value: 5%
Protein: 3 grams   Iron: 1 mg   Carbohydrate: 2 grams
Calcium: 17 mg   Dietary fiber: <1 gram

TOFU SPINACH DIP
(Serves 8)

1 large onion, finely chopped
2 cloves garlic, minced
2 Tablespoons oil
1/2 pound tofu, drained (soft or silken tofu is best)
3 Tablespoons mustard or eggless mayonnaise
10-ounce box frozen spinach, pre-cooked
Dash of pepper
Soy sauce or tamari to taste

Sauté onion and garlic in oil in a large frying pan over medium heat for 5 minutes. Pour into a blender cup and add remaining ingredients. Blend until creamy. Chill and serve with crackers and/or raw vegetables.

Total calories per serving: 67
Fat: 5 grams   Total Fat as % of Daily Value: 8%
Protein: 3 grams   Iron: 1 mg   Carbohydrate: 5 grams
Calcium: 69 mg   Dietary fiber: 1 gram

TOFU EGGLESS SALAD
(Serves 6)

1 pound tofu, drained and crumbled (firm tofu is best)
1 stalk celery, finely chopped
1 large carrot, grated
3 Tablespoons sweet pickle relish
2 Tablespoons eggless mayonnaise
Salt, pepper, and dill weed to taste

In a medium-size bowl mix all the ingredients together. Serve on a bed of lettuce or on whole grain toast with lettuce and sprouts.

Total calories per serving: 117
Fat: 6 grams   Total Fat as % of Daily Value: 9%
Protein: 9 grams   Iron: 1 mg   Carbohydrate: 6 grams
Calcium: 139 mg   Dietary fiber: 1 gram

SUMMER TOFU SALAD
(Serves 4)

1/2 pound romaine lettuce leaves, rinsed
1 pound tofu, drained and cut in finger-size pieces (soft or
    silken tofu is best)
1 stalk celery, chopped
2 scallions, chopped
1 large white radish, chopped
1/4 cup fresh parsley, finely chopped
1 large ripe tomato, chopped
1 Tablespoon soy sauce or tamari
1 teaspoon oil
Salt and pepper to taste

Lay lettuce leaves on 4 small plates. Arrange pieces of tofu around perimeter of each plate leaving an empty circle in the middle. Sprinkle with celery, scallions, radish, and parsley. Put tomato in center of each plate. Drizzle soy sauce or tamari and oil over the entire dish. Season and serve.

Hint: This salad tastes better if it sits a while before serving.

Total calories per serving: 98
Fat: 5 grams   Total Fat as % of Daily Value: 8%
Protein: 7 grams   Iron: 2 mg   Carbohydrate: 8 grams
Calcium: 69 mg   Dietary fiber: 2 grams

SPINACH PIE
(Serves 8)

10-ounce box frozen spinach
1-1/2 cups onion, chopped
3 cloves garlic, minced
2 Tablespoons oil
3 cups crumbled tofu (soft or silken tofu is best)
1 Tablespoon lemon juice
Salt and pepper to taste
1 pre-made pie crust

Cook spinach according to package directions. Sauté onion and garlic in oil in a large pot over medium heat for 3 minutes. Add spinach, tofu, lemon juice, and seasoning. Preheat oven to 350 degrees. Meanwhile, continue cooking spinach/tofu mixture for 5 minutes. Mix well. Pour into pie crust. Bake at 350 degrees for 15-20 minutes until crust is brown.

Total calories per serving: 180
Fat: 11 grams   Total Fat as % of Daily Value: 18%
Protein: 7 grams   Iron: 2 mg   Carbohydrate: 15 grams
Calcium: 87 mg   Dietary fiber: 1 gram

TOFU BURGERS
(Serves 4)

2 cups tofu, crumbled (firm tofu is best)
2 teaspoons garlic powder
1 cup wheat germ
2 teaspoons onion powder
2 Tablespoons soy sauce or tamari
1 teaspoon pepper
1/2 cup fresh parsley, finely chopped
1/2 cup celery, finely chopped
1 Tablespoon oil
1/2 cup water or vegetable broth
2 teaspoons oil for frying

Blend or mash tofu well and add remaining ingredients (except 2 teaspoons oil for frying). (The easiest way to do this is in a food processor, but you can do it by hand.) Mix well. Form patties and fry in a lightly oiled frying pan on both sides until brown (approximately 10 minutes). Serve warm on whole grain bread with lettuce and sliced tomato. Cold leftover burgers are also good.

Variation: Bake burgers instead of frying by first rolling patties in wheat germ. Lay in baking pan and bake at 350 degrees until warm and light brown.

Total calories per serving: 318
Fat: 16 grams   Total Fat as % of Daily Value: 25%
Protein: 24 grams   Iron: 5 mg   Carbohydrate: 19 grams
Calcium: 256 mg   Dietary fiber: <1 gram

FRIED TOFU
(Serves 4)

1 pound tofu, drained and sliced
1/4 cup soy sauce or tamari
1 cup unbleached white flour
2 Tablespoons oil
Salt and pepper to taste

Dip tofu in soy sauce or tamari, then in flour. Season well with salt and pepper, then fry in oil over medium heat in a large frying pan until brown on both sides (approximately 10-15 minutes). Serve warm as is or as a sandwich on whole grain bread with lettuce and tomato.

Variations: Instead of unbleached white flour, use wheat germ or nutritional yeast.

Total calories per serving: 271
Fat: 13 grams   Total Fat as % of Daily Value: 20%
Protein: 14 grams   Iron: 8 mg   Carbohydrate: 27 grams
Calcium: 127 mg   Dietary fiber: 1 gram

CURRIED TOFU WITH PEANUTS
(Serves 4)

1 large onion, finely chopped
2 cloves garlic, minced
3 Tablespoons oil
1/4 cup roasted peanuts, whole or chopped
1 pound tofu, drained and cut into 1-inch cubes
1 teaspoon salt
1 teaspoon curry powder
1-1/2 cup peas (fresh, frozen, or canned)
1 large carrot, chopped

Sauté onion and garlic in oil in large frying pan over medium heat for 3 minutes. Add remaining ingredients and cook for 15 minutes longer. Add a little water if necessary to prevent sticking. Serve warm over a bed of rice.

Variations: Use garlic powder or minced ginger instead of garlic. Also, use different nuts and vegetables.

Total calories per serving: 299
Fat: 20 grams   Total Fat as % of Daily Value: 30%
Protein: 15 grams   Iron: 7 mg   Carbohydrate: 18 grams
Calcium: 156 mg   Dietary fiber: 4 grams

FRIED TEMPEH SANDWICHES
(Serves 4)

8-ounce package tempeh (any variety), sliced into strips
2 Tablespoons oil
1 medium onion, chopped
Salt and pepper to taste
8 slices whole grain bread

Fry tempeh in oil with onions and seasoning over medium heat in a large frying pan until brown on both sides (approximately 10 minutes). Place tempeh and onions on whole grain bread with sliced tomato, cucumber, mayonnaise or mustard, sprouts, and lettuce.

Total calories per serving (not including tomato, etc.): 322
Fat: 14 grams   Total Fat as % of Daily Value: 22%
Protein: 16 grams   Iron: 3 mg   Carbohydrate: 38 grams
Calcium: 98 mg   Dietary fiber: <1 gram

SPAGHETTI AND TEMPEH SAUCE
(Serves 4)

1 pound spaghetti, pre-cooked and drained

Sauce:

8-ounce package tempeh (any variety), chopped into 1-inch cubes
1/2 teaspoon oregano
Garlic powder and salt to taste
1 small onion, finely chopped (optional)
2 Tablespoons oil
8-ounce can tomato sauce

Sauté tempeh in oil with seasoning and chopped onion if desired in a large frying pan over medium heat for 5 minutes. Add tomato sauce and heat 5 minutes longer. Serve warm over cooked spaghetti.

Total calories per serving: 408
Fat: 13 grams   Total Fat as % of Daily Value: 20%
Protein: 26 grams   Iron: 6 mg   Carbohydrate: 98 grams
Calcium: 80 mg   Dietary fiber: 1 gram

Chinese Cuisine

CHINESE MIXED VEGETABLES AND TOFU
(Serves 5)

2 Tablespoons oil
1/2 cup vegetable broth
**2 cups vegetables, chopped (i.e. celery, carrots, green
    pepper, bok choy, corn, snow peas)**
8 ounces tofu, drained and cubed (firm tofu is best)
Soy sauce or tamari to taste

Stir-fry ingredients in oil and broth in a large frying pan over medium heat for 15 minutes. Serve alone or over a bed of rice.

Total calories per serving (celery, carrots, green pepper, and bok choy): 115
Fat: 8 grams   Total Fat as % of Daily Value: 12%
Protein: 6 grams   Iron: 1 mg   Carbohydrate: 5 grams
Calcium: 93 mg   Dietary fiber: 1 gram

STIR-FRIED VEGETABLES, GINGER, AND RICE
(Serves 6)

1 Tablespoon oil
1/3 cup vegetable broth
3 cups mixed vegetables, chopped
1-1/2 cups pre-cooked rice (leftovers are good)
2 Tablespoons soy sauce or tamari
1/4 teaspoon fresh ginger, grated

Sauté vegetables in oil and broth in a large pot over medium heat for 10 minutes. Add rice, soy sauce or tamari, and ginger to vegetables. Cook 8 minutes longer and serve warm.

Total calories per serving (using broccoli, carrots, and cabbage): 96
Fat: 3 grams   Total Fat as % of Daily Value: 5%
Protein: 3 grams   Iron: 1 mg   Carbohydrate: 16 grams
Calcium: 25 mg   Dietary fiber: 2 grams

VEGETABLE CHOW MEIN
(Serves 6)

2 Tablespoons oil
1/2 cup vegetable broth
3 cups pre-cooked rice (leftovers are good)
1 cup bean sprouts (fresh or canned)
1 stalk celery, chopped
1 large green pepper, chopped
1 large carrot, chopped
2 large ripe tomatoes, chopped
Soy sauce or tamari to taste

Sauté the rice and vegetables with soy sauce or tamari in oil and broth in a large frying pan over medium heat for 15 minutes. Serve warm.

Total calories per serving: 176
Fat: 6 grams   Total Fat as % of Daily Value: 9%
Protein: 3 grams   Iron: 1 mg   Carbohydrate: 29 grams
Calcium: 23 mg   Dietary fiber: 3 grams

MOCK FOO YOUNG
(Serves 2)

10 ounces tofu, crumbled (firm tofu is best)
1/4 cup cornmeal
1 large carrot, grated
Salt and pepper to taste
1/4 teaspoon oregano
1 Tablespoon sesame seeds (optional)
2 teaspoons oil for frying

Blend all the ingredients (except oil for frying) together in a blender. Form four patties and fry on both sides until light brown in a lightly oiled frying pan over medium heat.

Variation: For a totally different taste, cover patties with tomato sauce and sprinkle with vegan cheese.

Total calories per serving: 288
Fat: 13 grams   Total Fat as % of Daily Value: 20%
Protein: 18 grams   Iron: 3 mg   Carbohydrate: 16 grams
Calcium: 260 mg   Dietary fiber: 2 grams

FRIED RICE WITH PEANUTS OR ALMONDS
(Serves 6)

1 large onion, chopped
1 Tablespoon oil
2 cups pre-cooked rice (leftovers are good)
1 large green pepper, chopped
1 stalk celery, chopped
1 cup mushrooms, sliced
1 small zucchini, chopped
2 Tablespoons soy sauce or tamari
1 cup roasted peanuts or almonds, chopped or whole

Sauté onion in oil in a large frying pan over a medium heat for 3 minutes. Add the remaining ingredients and stir-fry 15 minutes.

Total calories per serving: 256
Fat: 15 grams   Total Fat as % of Daily Value: 23%
Protein: 9 grams   Iron: 1 mg   Carbohydrate: 25 grams
Calcium: 42 mg   Dietary fiber: 4 grams

Mexican Fiesta

MEXICAN SUCCOTASH
(Serves 6)

2 Tablespoons oil
1 small onion, chopped
1 pound zucchini, sliced
1 large green pepper, chopped
1/4 cup pimientos, diced
2 large ripe tomatoes, chopped
1-1/2 cups corn kernels (frozen, fresh, or canned)
Salt and pepper to taste

Sauté onion in oil in a large frying pan over medium heat for 3 minutes. Add remaining ingredients and simmer until vegetables are tender (about 10 minutes). Add a little water if necessary to prevent sticking. Serve as a side dish or over a bed of rice.

Total calories per serving: 112
Fat: 5 grams   Total Fat as % of Daily Value: 8%
Protein: 3 grams   Iron: 1 mg   Carbohydrate: 8 grams
Calcium: 18 mg   Dietary fiber: 3 grams

REFRIED BEANS
(Serves 8)

1 large onion, chopped
3 Tablespoons oil
Two 15-ounce cans pinto or kidney beans, drained
6-ounce can tomato paste
3 Tablespoons chili powder

Sauté onion in oil in a large frying pan over a medium heat for three minutes. Add the remaining ingredients and stir-fry for 15 minutes. Serve over tortilla chips or in taco shells with shredded lettuce, chopped tomatoes, hot sauce, olives, etc.

Total calories per serving: 162
Fat: 6 grams   Total Fat as % of Daily Value: 9%
Protein: 6 grams   Iron: 3 mg   Carbohydrate: 22 grams
Calcium: 57 mg   Dietary fiber: 2 grams

EASY TOSTADAS
(Serves 6-8)

Two 1-pound cans vegetarian chili
1 box vegan enchilada shells or flat taco shells
1 cup shredded lettuce
1 large cucumber, peeled and chopped
1 large onion, chopped
1/2 cup shredded vegan cheese (optional)
Taco sauce to taste

Heat chili in a large pot until warm. Preheat oven to 400 degrees. Lay shells in a single layer on a cookie sheet. Spread chili on each shell. Heat at 400 degrees for 5 minutes. Remove from oven and let each person garnish shells with remaining ingredients as desired. Note: This dish tastes good chilled as well. Simply open can and put chili on shells and garnish. This is a terrific dish when traveling.

Total calories per serving: 278
Fat: 2 grams   Total Fat as % of Daily Value: 3%
Protein: 15 grams   Iron: 4 mg   Carbohydrate: 51 grams
Calcium: 103 mg   Dietary fiber: 13 grams

GUACAMOLE
(Serves 4)

1 large or 2 small ripe avocados, peeled and pit(s) removed
1 small ripe tomato, finely chopped
1/4 teaspoon garlic powder
Pinch of cayenne pepper
Salt to taste

Mash avocado in a bowl. Add chopped tomato and seasonings. Mix well and serve on tacos, with chips or crackers, or as a dip with raw vegetables.

Total calories per serving: 100
Fat: 9 grams   Total Fat as % of Daily Value: 14%
Protein: 1 gram   Iron: 1 mg   Carbohydrate: 5 grams
Calcium: 7 mg   Dietary fiber: 2 grams

Spreads and Dips

Spreads can be used for parties, snacks, or light dinners. They not only taste good, but can be nutritious. But like many foods, if you eat too much, the calories will add up. Serve these spreads and dips with lowfat crackers, breads, or raw vegetables such as carrots, celery, peppers, cauliflower, or zucchini.

LENTIL PATE
(Serves 8)

1 cup lentils
2 cups water
1 large onion, finely chopped
4 cloves garlic, minced
1 Tablespoon margarine
1 teaspoon black pepper
1/2 teaspoon vinegar
Water if necessary

Cook lentils in water in a medium-size pot until done. At the same time, sauté onions and garlic in margarine in a separate pot over medium heat for 3 minutes. Add pepper. Mix lentils, onions, garlic, and pepper together. Blend the mixture in a food processor adding water if necessary until well mixed. Add vinegar last. Chill before serving.

Total calories per serving: 85
Fat: 2 grams   Total Fat as % of Daily Value: 3%
Protein: 5 grams   Iron: 2 mg   Carbohydrate: 13 grams
Calcium: 17 mg   Dietary fiber: 3 grams

MUSHROOM/EGGPLANT SPREAD
(Makes about 4 cups)

1 pound eggplant, peeled and chopped into 1-inch cubes
12 ounces portabello mushrooms, finely chopped
Medium onion, finely chopped
2 Tablespoons oil
1/2 teaspoon coriander
1/2 teaspoon cumin
Salt and pepper to taste

Sauté ingredients in a large frying pan over medium-high heat for 10-12 minutes. Mash with a potato masher until a chunky, yet spreadable consistency. Chill and spread on crackers or bread.

Total calories per ¼ cup serving: 30
Fat: 2 grams   Total Fat as % of Daily Value: 3%
Protein: 1 gram   Iron: <1 mg   Carbohydrate: 3 grams
Calcium: 4 mg   Dietary fiber: <1 gram

GARBANZO PEANUT SPREAD
(Serves 8)

16-ounce can chickpeas, drained
3 Tablespoons peanut butter
1/3 cup lemon juice
3/4 cup water or as needed
1 Tablespoon oil
1/8 teaspoon cumin
1/2 teaspoon garlic powder
Salt and pepper to taste

Blend all the ingredients together in a food processor until smooth. Add more water if necessary.

Variation: Instead of using peanut butter, use tahini (sesame butter) and add some sautéed onions and parsley.

Total calories per serving: 125
Fat: 6 grams   Total Fat as % of Daily Value: 9%
Protein: 5 grams   Iron: 1 mg   Carbohydrate: 14 grams
Calcium: 27 mg   Dietary fiber: 5 grams

SPLIT PEA SPREAD
(Serves 6)

1 cup split peas
3-1/4 cups water
1 large carrot, finely chopped
2 stalks celery, finely chopped
1 small onion, finely chopped
1 teaspoon celery seed
Salt and pepper to taste

Bring split peas to a rapid boil in a medium-size pot. Add carrot and celery. Then add onions and seasoning. Cover pot and boil 15 minutes longer. Remove from heat and blend until smooth in a food processor. Place in a bowl and chill before serving.

Total calories per serving: 125
Fat: <1 gram   Total Fat as % of Daily Value: <1%
Protein: 8 grams   Iron: 2 mg   Carbohydrate: 23 grams
Calcium: 30 mg   Dietary fiber: 2 grams

CHOPPED "LIVER" SPREAD
(Serves 6)

1 Tablespoon oil
1/4 cup water
1/2 pound mushrooms, chopped
1 small onion, chopped
1 cup chopped walnuts
Salt and pepper to taste

Sauté mushrooms and onion in oil and water in a large frying pan over medium heat for 8 minutes. Pour into a food processor. Add walnuts and seasoning. Blend until smooth, adding more water if necessary. Chill before serving.

Total calories per serving: 115
Fat: 10 grams   Total Fat as % of Daily Value: 17%
Protein: 4 grams   Iron: 1 mg   Carbohydrate: 4 grams
Calcium: 12 mg   Dietary fiber: 1 gram

WHITE BEAN SPREAD
(Makes about 2 cups)

19-ounce can white beans, drained
1 stalk celery, finely chopped
Juice of 1/2 small lemon
1/4 teaspoon dill weed
Pepper to taste

Mash white beans in a bowl. Add remaining ingredients and mix well. Chill before serving.

Total calories per ¼ cup serving: 78
Fat: <1 gram   Total Fat as % of Daily Value: <1%
Protein: 5 grams   Iron: 1 mg   Carbohydrate: 14 grams
Calcium: 34 mg   Dietary fiber: 3 grams

AVOCADO/CUCUMBER SPREAD
(Serves 8)

1 small ripe avocado, pit removed
1 large cucumber, peeled and chopped
1/4 teaspoon garlic powder
1/4 teaspoon salt
1/4 teaspoon cayenne

Place all the ingredients in a food processor and blend until creamy. This spread can also be used as a salad dressing.

Total calories per serving: 35
Fat: 3 grams   Total Fat as % of Daily Value: 5%
Protein: 1 gram   Iron: <1 mg   Carbohydrate: 2 grams
Calcium: 8 mg   Dietary fiber: 1 gram

NUT "CHEESE"
(Serves 6)

1/2 cup raw cashews
1/2 cup water
1/4 cup lemon juice
3 Tablespoons oil
1/2 small tomato, finely chopped
Garlic powder and paprika to taste

Blend cashews, water, and lemon juice together in a food processor. Slowly add oil. Then add remaining ingredients and blend well. Chill before serving.

Total calories per serving: 130
Fat: 12 grams   Total Fat as % of Daily Value: 18%
Protein: 2 grams   Iron: 1 mg   Carbohydrate: 5 grams
Calcium: 7 mg   Dietary fiber: 1 gram

Desserts

SPICY DATE NUT SPREAD
(Serves 4)

1/4 pound dates, pitted
1/2 cup hot water
1/2 cup walnuts, chopped
1 large apple, cored and finely chopped
1/4 teaspoon cinnamon
Pinch of ginger powder (optional)

Soak dates in hot water for a few minutes. Put date/water mixture in a food processor. Add remaining ingredients and blend until smooth. Serve on slices of fresh fruit including apples, peaches, and pears.

Total calories per serving: 169
Fat: 6 grams   Total Fat as % of Daily Value: 9%
Protein: 3 grams   Iron: 1 mg   Carbohydrate: 30 grams
Calcium: 19 mg   Dietary fiber: 4 grams

COCONUT CLUSTERS
(Serves 8)

2 cups shredded coconut
4 ripe medium bananas, mashed
1/4 cup cocoa powder or carob powder
1 cup walnuts, chopped (optional)

Preheat oven to 350 degrees. Blend ingredients together in a medium-size bowl. Form clusters on a lightly oiled cookie sheet. Bake for 20 minutes at 350 degrees. Cool, then remove from cookie sheet.

Variation: Instead of cocoa or carob powder, use 1/2 cup chopped fresh fruit such as strawberries.

Total calories per serving: 174
Fat: 9 grams   Total Fat as % of Daily Value: 14%
Protein: 2 grams   Iron: 2 mg   Carbohydrate: 26 grams
Calcium: 11 mg   Dietary fiber: 2 grams

OATMEAL COOKIES
(Makes 40 cookies)

1/2 cup vegan margarine
1-1/2 cups (15 ounces) applesauce
1/2 cup molasses or maple syrup
2 large ripe bananas, peeled
1-3/4 cups whole wheat pastry flour
1 teaspoon baking soda
1 teaspoon baking powder
1 teaspoon cinnamon
1 teaspoon nutmeg
3 cups rolled oats
1/2 cup raisins or chopped dates

Preheat oven to 400 degrees. Cream together margarine, applesauce, molasses or maple syrup, and bananas in a large bowl. Add remaining ingredients and mix well. Drop a rounded tablespoon of batter at a time on a lightly oiled cookie sheet. Bake 8 minutes at 400 degrees. Allow to cool before removing from cookie sheet.

Variation: Add chopped walnuts or chopped apples to batter.

Total calories per cookie: 84
Fat: 3 grams   Total Fat as % of Daily Value: 5%
Protein: 2 grams   Iron: 1 mg   Carbohydrate: 15 grams
Calcium: 24 mg   Dietary fiber: 1 gram

FRESH FRUIT SALAD AND PEANUT CREME
(Serves 8)

Prepare a fruit salad for 8 people using your favorite fruits in season. If you are in a rush, use canned fruit salad.

Peanut Creme:

1 cup water
2 apples
1 cup peanuts

Blend apples in 1/2 cup water in a food processor. Slowly add peanuts and remaining water as needed until a smooth consistency is reached. Serve over fruit salad.

Total calories per serving (without fruit): 125
Fat: 9 grams   Total Fat as % of Daily Value: 14%
Protein: 5 grams   Iron: <1 mg   Carbohydrate: 9 grams
Calcium: 18 mg   Dietary fiber: 2 grams

Variations: Serve peanut creme over baked apples and pears. You can also experiment with different types of nuts.

RICE PUDDING
(Serves 6)

1 cup rice
2/3 cups raisins
2 large ripe bananas, peeled and mashed
1/2 cup water
1 teaspoon cinnamon
1/4 teaspoon nutmeg

Cook rice with raisins following package instructions in a large pot until done. Preheat oven to 350 degrees. Pour cooked rice and raisins into a food processor. Add the remaining ingredients and blend together for 1 minute. Pour into a medium-size baking dish. Bake for 20 minutes at 350 degrees. Serve warm or chilled.

Total calories per serving: 209
Fat: <1 gram   Total Fat as % of Daily Value: <1%
Protein: 3 grams   Iron: 2 mg   Carbohydrate: 50 grams
Calcium: 14 mg   Dietary fiber: 2 grams

TOFU PIE AND QUICK CRUST
(Serves 8)

Pie crust:

2 cups lowfat granola
1/4 cup vegan margarine

Preheat oven to 350 degrees. Blend granola and margarine together in a medium-size bowl. Press into 8-inch pie pan and bake for 10 minutes at 350 degrees. Leave oven on while you prepare pie filling below.

Pie filling:

4 dates
1 pound tofu, drained (soft or silken tofu is best)
3 Tablespoons chocolate syrup
2 Tablespoons oil

Soak dates in a little boiling water for 5 minutes and drain. Place pie filling ingredients in a blender cup and blend until creamy, adding a little water if necessary.

Pour filling into pie crust and bake for 20 minutes at 350 degrees. Chill in the refrigerator before serving.

Variation: Instead of chocolate syrup use fresh chopped fruit such as strawberries, peaches, or blueberries.

Total calories per serving: 231
Fat: 12 grams   Total Fat as % of Daily Value: 18%
Protein: 6 grams   Iron: 2 mg   Carbohydrate: 28 grams
Calcium: 30 mg   Dietary fiber: 2 grams

Seasonal Party Ideas for Twelve People

SUMMERTIME MENU:

Fruit Salad (recipe below)

2 dozen bagels and/or rolls with vegan cream cheese (such as *Tofutti* brand) or vegan margarine

Raw Vegetable Platter (see page 162)

Guacamole (see page 151) or Avocado/Cucumber Spread (see page 156)

2 pounds assortment of nuts and seeds

2 pounds variety of dried fruit

2 gallons fruit juices and/or Blended Fruit Drink (see page 104)

1-1/2 dozen ears hot steamed corn (can be done indoors or outdoors over a barbecue)

FRUIT SALAD
(Serves 12)

1/2 ripe watermelon, cut lengthwise
10 peaches, pits removed and quartered
1 pint strawberries, sliced
1 pint blueberries
1 cup raisins
1 cup shredded coconut (optional)

Scoop out bite-size pieces of watermelon and place in a large bowl. Add remaining ingredients. Mix well and pour back into hollowed out watermelon shell. Keep chilled until serving.

Total calories per serving: 126
Fat: 1 gram   Total Fat as % of Daily Value: 2%
Protein: 2 grams   Iron: 1 mg   Carbohydrate: 31 grams
Calcium: 24 mg   Dietary fiber: 4 grams

RAW VEGETABLE PLATTER
(Serves 12)

5 large ripe tomatoes, sliced
1 pound carrots, sliced lengthwise into sticks
3 cucumbers, peeled and sliced
4 stalks celery, sliced lengthwise into sticks
1 pound olives, drained
1 pound chopped broccoli or cauliflower
1 pound zucchini, sliced lengthwise into sticks

Arrange all the vegetables on a large platter.

Total calories per serving: 120
Fat: 9 grams   Total Fat as % of Daily Value: 14%
Protein: 4 grams   Iron: 2 mg   Carbohydrate: 14 grams
Calcium: 91 mg   Dietary fiber: 5 grams

AUTUMN MENU:

Creamed Carrot Soup (see page 116 and double the recipe)
Ratatouille (see page 136 and double the recipe)
4 cups rice precooked
Curried Tofu with Peanuts (see page 144 and triple the recipe)
1 dozen fresh apples (assorted colors if possible)
2 gallons apple cider or apple juice
Oatmeal cookies (see page 158)

WINTER MENU:

Vegetarian Chili (see page 135 and triple the recipe)
24 taco shells
2 large bags corn chips
Small head lettuce, shredded
1 pound vegan cheese, shredded
2 large onions, finely chopped
Large bottle hot sauce
12 large baked potatoes
Hot Apple Cider (see page 104 and double the recipe)
Coconut Clusters (see page 157 and double the recipe)

SPRING MENU:

Tofu Eggless Salad (see page 140 and double the recipe)
Mock "Tuna" Salad (see page 118 and double the recipe)
Cucumber Salad (see page 108 and double the recipe)
2 large boxes vegan bread sticks
White Bean Spread (see page 155 and double the recipe)
2 large loaves whole wheat bread and 1-1/2 dozen rolls
6 tangerines
6 oranges
6 large bananas
2 pints strawberries
6 apples
2 gallons assorted fruit juices

Vegetarian/Vegan Meal Plan

If you are in doubt about your diet, you can use this plan prepared by Ruth Blackburn, R.D. as a <u>GENERAL GUIDE</u>. Consult a dietitian or medical doctor knowledgeable about nutrition if you have a special problem.

A. PROTEIN FOODS: 1-2 SERVINGS PER DAY

1. one serving equals:
> 1-1/2 cups cooked dried beans or peas
> 8 ounces tofu*
> 4 ounces tempeh
> 2 cups fortified soy milk*
> 1/2 cup almonds*, cashews, walnuts, pecans
> 1/4 cup peanuts
> 4 Tablespoons peanut butter
> 2 cups lowfat milk or yogurt*
> 2 ounces cheese*
> 1/2 cup cottage cheese*
> 2 eggs

B. WHOLE GRAINS: AT LEAST 6-8 SERVINGS/DAY

1. one serving equals:
> 1 slice whole wheat, rye, or whole grain bread
> 1 buckwheat or whole wheat pancake or waffle
> 1 two-inch piece cornbread
> 2 Tablespoons wheat germ
> 1 ounce wheat or oat bran
> 1/4 cup sunflower*, sesame*, or pumpkin seeds
> 3/4 cup wheat, bran, or corn flakes
> 1/2 cup oatmeal or farina
> 1/2 cup cooked brown rice, barley, bulgur, or corn
> 1/2 cup whole wheat noodles, macaroni, or spaghetti

C. VEGETABLES: AT LEAST 4-6 SERVINGS/DAY

1. two or more servings/day of the following:

    1/2 cup cooked or 1 cup raw broccoli*, Brussels sprouts, collards*, kale*, chard, spinach, romaine, cabbage, carrots, sweet potatoes, winter squash, tomatoes

2. two or more servings/day (1 serving equals 1/2 cup cooked or 1 cup raw) of any other vegetable

D. FRUITS: 4-6 SERVINGS/DAY

1. two servings/day of the following:

    3/4 cup berries, 1/4 cantaloupe, 1 orange, 1/2 grapefruit, 1 lemon or lime, 1/2 papaya, 4-inch x 8-inch watermelon slice, or 1/2 cup orange, grapefruit, or vitamin C enriched juice

2. two to four servings/day of other fruits:

    1 small piece fresh fruit
    3/4 cup grapes
    1/2 cup cooked fruit or canned fruit without sugar
    2 Tablespoons raisins, dates, or dried fruit

E. FATS: 0-4 SERVINGS/DAY

1. one serving equals:

    1 teaspoon margarine, butter, or oil
    2 teaspoons mayonnaise or salad dressing
    1 Tablespoon cream cheese, gravy, or cream sauce

F. STARRED * FOOD ITEMS: 2, 3, OR MORE SERVINGS/DAY

1. Men include 2 choices daily as a source of calcium
2. Women include 3 choices daily as a source of calcium

G. EXCEPTIONS

1. Pregnant women, persons under 18, and persons with bone or muscle trauma or other special needs may require additional servings.

2. Vegans (vegetarians who also don't use dairy products and eggs) need to include a vitamin B-12 source regularly. Sources include: some brands of nutritional yeast and vitamin fortified foods such as Grape-Nuts cereal and Pillsbury's Green Giant Harvest Burgers.

SAMPLE TWO DAY MENU

	BREAKFAST	LUNCH	DINNER	SNACKS

DAY 1	French toast
	Orange juice
		Split pea soup
		Biscuits
		Celery with
		  vegan cream
		  cheese
		Fresh fruit
			Tomato eggplant bake
			Macaroni, peas, and
			  corn
			Pear halves
				Graham
				  cracker
				Milk or forti-
				  fied soy milk

DAY 2	Bran, corn, or
	  wheat flakes
	  and milk or
	  soy milk
	Banana
		Peanut butter
		  and sliced
		  apples on
		  whole wheat
		  bread
		Carrot/raisin
		  salad
			Cheese or tofu omelet
			  with vegetables
			Wheat toast
			Steamed broccoli
			Baked potato
				Ginger snaps
				Lemonade

Vegetarianism on the Job

A common problem vegetarians encounter is finding something to eat at work. Cafeterias often offer very little food that we can consume besides salads or perhaps yogurt. As a result, vegetarians must often bring their own lunch. What happens when you have to attend a business luncheon or travel? The following essays are true stories written by those in the working world who have learned to cope in a primarily meat-eating society. We also include ideas for adults whose job is to raise children.

COMPUTER PROGRAMMER

I work in a building with 300 employees, so our cafeteria has limited selections (almost all of which are not vegan). To save time, I bring my lunch to work every day rather than go out.

I don't like to spend a lot of time during the week preparing lunches, so I try to do any cooking on the weekend. I prepare double or triple batches of vegetarian chili, split pea soup, black bean soup, or lentil soup. Then I freeze individual portions. During the week, I grab one of the items from the freezer and add an apple, a microwaved potato, or half a sandwich. I'll also take leftover spaghetti.

Fortunately, I have a bread machine, which makes preparing delicious whole wheat vegan breads easy. I'll make a loaf on Sunday night and it lasts me throughout the week. Sometimes, I'll also use leftover bagels for lunch that I have put in the freezer.

When I don't take the time to cook in advance, I'll go for convenience foods such as Fantastic Foods Cha-Cha Chili or Five Bean Soup or Cascadian Farms frozen Meals in a Minute. These meals are bags of frozen organic rice and bean mixtures in various flavors such as Indian, Mexican, or Moroccan. You simply add boiling water or heat them up.

REGISTERED DIETITIAN

I've been a nutritionist for over 17 years, but I've been a vegetarian much longer. You would think that vegetarianism would be more prevalent among those who make diet and health their business, but that's not the case.

I'm non-traditional among those in my profession in another way, too. I have a home-based business and make my living as a nutrition consultant. Most of my time is spent in my home office, sitting at my desk, phoning, faxing, and word processing on my computer. My schedule is my own, and that means that I may eat breakfast, lunch, and dinner at times that may be totally out of sync with the outside world.

Others may not see what I eat when I'm working at home, but I keep myself in line. I spend very little time preparing lunch — under 10 minutes — because I'm busy and like to get back to work quickly. Sometimes I heat up leftovers from dinner the night before. Examples may be a slice or two of cheeseless vegetable pizza, a serving of a bean and vegetable casserole, or leftover Chinese take-out. I also like to reheat plain leftover vegetables (especially steamed kale or sweet potatoes) and I eat that with a couple of slices of whole wheat toast and a glass of orange juice. Sometimes I buy fresh carrot juice from the supermarket and mix that with orange juice. It's a delicious blend, and it always seems like a magically healthful "elixir" to me. I don't skimp when it comes to good quality food, and I keep a wide variety on hand.

On the other hand, I've also been known to have a bowl of cereal with soy milk for lunch, especially when I have a favorite kind in the cupboard. I'm a big fan of cereal (dry or hot). Sometimes I even eat it for dessert. Other days, I may cook a potato in the microwave and eat it with ketchup or salsa along with a toasted bagel or English muffin. Another favorite is a sweet potato cooked in the microwave, then topped with a little brown sugar and several "squeezes" of fresh lime juice.

I usually have hummus in my 'fridge, so some days I'll eat that in whole grain pita pockets. Another staple is a bag of baby carrots (the kind that are already peeled), and I'll eat a handful of those, dipped in hummus, along with a peanut butter and banana sandwich. Another common lunch is a big pasta bowl filled with mesclun salad mix. I add about a half cup of garbanzo beans, sliced tomatoes (if they're in season), a few black olives, and some ground black pepper. I top it with flavored vinegar (mango or raspberry vinegar are my favorites). I eat a slice of toast with that, or a piece of fresh fruit.

I care about the quality and presentation of my food. I eat a lot of plain, fresh foods prepared very simply. I take care to make my plate look attractive and even add a garnish now and then — even though it's only me who sees it! I may not spend much time preparing my meals, but I eat very well and enjoy my food immensely.

TEST STATISTICIAN

In the summer I bring cut up fresh tomatoes and make a lettuce and tomato sandwich on whole wheat bread that I bring from home. Otherwise, I eat at the salad bar at work.

During the winter months, I bring hummus, baba ghanouj, or fat-free cream cheese and tomato sandwiches on whole wheat bread. When I'm rushed I have to resort to the salad bar at work. I may also bring leftover baked potatoes that I microwave. This is typical. On occasion, when I have leftover pasta salads from home, I'll bring that, too.

MUSIC THEORIST AND ADMINISTRATOR

I bring a 1/2 cup of cottage cheese, 2 cups popcorn, and half an apple to work for lunch. I'll also bring a caffeine-free diet soda. (About once a week I go buy a cookie, too!)

SPORTS WRITER/EDITOR

When I eat lunch, I'm usually at one of three locations: home, an office, or a sporting event. If I'm at home, I may eat small snacks all day (fruit, granola, peanut butter and crackers, etc.) and work right through lunch. If I do sit down to lunch at home, it's frequently comprised of the previous evening's leftovers. I keep whole wheat pitas and tortillas handy at all times and will usually fill a pita or roll a tortilla with leftover grains, vegetables, crumbled tofu or tempeh. Then I just heat and eat. Sometimes, I'll also spread hummus or refried beans on the pita or tortilla and once in a while I'll have a salad or bowl of hot soup on the side.

If I'm at one of the offices where I occasionally work, I might bring some leftovers, a sandwich or a packaged cup of soup or pasta. If not, I'll get a sandwich at a nearby deli or sub shop. A couple of slices of whole wheat bread loaded with vegetables and some hot peppers is a favorite. A few nearby restaurants serve veggie burgers, so I make that an occasional choice. Take-out orders from nearby Thai, Chinese, Italian, Indian, or Mexican eateries fit easily into my eating style. One of my favorite take-out items is a pizza covered with tomato sauce and basil, and dotted with chunks of falafel. Admittedly, you won't find this option at most pizza places, but if you love falafel, you should try creating this work of art at home.

Most of the sporting events I cover are at night, so I'm usually scrambling for dinner options on those evenings. From time to time I do find myself at a matinee hockey game. The home team provides a free meal to the working press two or three hours before game time. Usually this meal consists of the dead critter of the day accompanied by some form of potato, some overly steamed vegetables, a skimpy iceberg lettuce salad, and white rolls. Doesn't exactly make your taste buds dance, does it? If pressed for time, I might suffer through the wilted veggies, the salad, and the potatoes. But more often I'll pack a sandwich and some fruit to eat or try to eat a light lunch at a nearby restaurant. Another option is eating a large, late breakfast and bringing along fruit, granola, crackers, and other light snack items.

EDUCATIONAL TESTING SPECIALIST

I generally have a salad from the salad bar in our cafeteria or two to three hot side dishes such as rice with Brussels sprouts or kale, baked potatoes, or mushrooms. I also eat peanut butter and jelly sandwiches, or cheese and onion, or lettuce, tomato, and onion sandwiches. Sometimes I have a slice of pizza or a dish of macaroni and cheese. I also like to bring celery and carrot sticks or an apple for snacks (when I remember to cut up the veggies).

EDUCATION RESEARCHER

I don't like to cook and I don't have a lot of time in the morning to put a bag lunch together. My lunch consists of putting my hand in my freezer and pulling out a Veggie Pocket — they come in seven different varieties. I throw a handful of baby carrots in a plastic bag (which I reuse) and take a piece of fruit or two: apples and pears in the fall and winter; peaches and plums in the summer. At lunchtime, I just pop my Veggie Pocket in the microwave for 90 seconds and voila, lunch!

MATHEMATICIAN

I used to have hummus on pita bread and sometimes yogurt or salad. Occasionally, I'll bring vegetarian cup-of-soups where you can add water and microwave them or add boiling water.

Lately I've been having peanut butter crackers or cheese crackers, and a granola bar and juice. I don't typically eat a lot for lunch and I go through different phases.

ACCOUNTANT

My first job after graduating from college was for an accounting firm. At previous jobs, and throughout my life as a student, my vegetarian lifestyle was not a problem to deal with on a daily basis. I either brought my lunch with me or I ate at a place that I knew had vegetarian options available. While working for the accounting firm, however, I was often forced to be more flexible with my eating habits.

Most of the time, I worked at our clients' places of business. Therefore, I was not able to bring my lunch and I often had to go out to eat. Fortunately, I was often able to eat a decent meal. Other times, I needed to be a bit more creative with what I ordered for lunch. On several occasions, I worked at businesses located in small towns that had only one or two eating places. Most of these places were sandwich shops or family restaurants whose only vegetarian options were cheese subs or salads. It was during this time that I began to order what I call a PLT sandwich. This is made of peppers, lettuce, and tomato with the occasional addition of mushrooms when they are available. During one engagement, the only place where we could eat was at this little sandwich shop on the corner across the street. They had a selection of bagel sandwiches, all of which had meat or cheese on them. I ended up asking if they could make me a bagel sandwich with lettuce, tomatoes, and mushrooms. I was amazed at how ordering these sandwiches could cause such a crisis for the people who worked in the restaurant. In the end, however, no one ever denied me my "special orders" and many times I ended up getting a great bargain on the price. One woman who waited on me actually said she might like to try a PLT and that they would even consider adding it to their menu!

My co-workers were often curious about my lifestyle. Initially, a few of them would make sarcastic comments, attempting to make me get angry and defensive about my beliefs. After getting past the "Vegan, what is that?" stage, I believe most of my co-workers have grown to realize that stereotypes are nothing more than blatant generalizations. For just as not every accountant is a boring pocket-protector wearing businessperson, not every vegetarian looks down upon meat-eating people. As my co-workers learned more about my lifestyle choices, many of them grew to respect me for standing up for what I believe. At the same time, there will always be some people who have absolutely no interest in vegetarianism and I will always respect their freedom to choose their lifestyle. I have learned that the best way for vegetarians to educate others about vegetarianism is to simply live our lives according to our beliefs. There is no good reason to force our opinions on other people. If someone is curious about vegetarianism, they will approach us.

In general, the more often I ate in restaurants, the more I came to realize that there definitely are options available for both vegetarians and vegans. The key to discovering these options is to ask. Although the number of vegetarians is increasing, the majority of people are not vegetarian and menus are merely a reflection of this. However, most restaurants are quite willing to accommodate vegetarians. Regardless of our dietary preferences, we are still paying customers. With creativity and flexibility, eating out while on the job is actually quite simple. I have never expected to be able to order tempeh stroganoff or tofu cheesecake, but I have not had a problem ordering a salad with a baked potato, a few fruit cups to make a fruit salad, or a few side dishes of vegetables for a lunch platter. The best way vegetarians can encourage a restaurant to offer vegetarian dishes on their menu is to continue to request them. Only then can we expect to see more changes.

PARENTS

Lunchtimes are often not sit-down affairs, at least not for me. With two young children stating, "Could I please have more soy milk," "I want (whatever mom is eating," and of course, "I'm through and I need my hands washed (right as mom sits down to eat)" are some of the usual sounds.

So, my criteria for lunch foods are those that are quick to prepare. When my children were younger, I ate a lot of peanut butter. It was quick, it was filling, and it was often what I was fixing for them. We ate PB on bagels (cinnamon raisin bagels are best), PB sandwiches, PB on bananas, and PB on apples. Oh, yes, PB on crackers, too.

Leftovers, are another good, quick lunch. I usually try to have leftovers from dinner as one lunch option. They're often eaten straight out of the refrigerator or they can be reheated in a microwave. My personal favorites are soups, cold vegetables, and pasta.

I often make shakes for the children and may have some myself. These are made by combining half a package of silken soft tofu, some soy milk, a frozen banana or other fruit (strawberries, blueberries, peaches, applesauce, etc.), and maple syrup to taste in the food processor. Leftover frozen dessert (sorbet, Rice Dream, etc.) can also be added. These are good with bread or crackers on the side.

Hummus or some other kind of bean dip is also pretty quick. I eat this in pita bread, with crackers, on a bagel, or with vegetables and apples as dippers.

In the summer, my favorite lunch is a sliced tomato, still warm from the garden, on whole-grain bread or a bagel with spicy mustard. I could live on this!

If breakfast was a hurried affair, I may have a bowl of cold cereal with soy milk and fruit or some oatmeal for lunch. This is always amusing to the children.

My husband is also home during the day. His favorite quick lunches are leftovers, Tofu Pups, and Harvest Burgers. He always takes advantage of the garden in the summer and has veggie sandwiches and salads. And of course, there are the "immediate leftovers" from the children—crusts, rejected special of the day, and anything designated as "yucky."

On the next two pages you will find a chart listing a sample of nutrients found in various foods. You can find tables for common food items in the USDA *Home and Garden Bulletin Number 72 Nutritive Values of Foods*. This book is appropriate for most consumer uses and is available at <http:\\www.nal.usda.gov/fnic/foodcomp>. More extensive information can be found in the USDA *Handbook Number 8*. Both of these handbooks can be purchased from the National Technical Information Service, 5285 Port Royal Rd., Springfield, VA 22161. The cookbook *Laurel's Kitchen* also has very useful nutrition information and can be purchased from The Vegetarian Resource Group, PO Box 1463, Baltimore, MD 21203 or by calling VRG at (410) 366-8343.

The Recommended Daily Allowances (RDA) are the amounts of nutrients recommended by the Food and Nutrition Board, and are considered adequate for maintenance of good nutrition in healthy persons in the United States.

Please note that in an equal amount of calories, greens such as kale and collards have more calcium, iron, and protein than beef. The key to a healthy vegetarian diet is to eat a wide variety of foods. If you were eating only meat and no vegetables, you would have a hard time meeting your dietary needs.

TURN PAGE FOR NUTRIENT CHART!

Nutrient Chart

FOOD	AMOUNT	CALORIES	PROTEIN (g)	CALCIUM (mg)	IRON (mg)
Cottage cheese					
2% lowfat	1 cup	203	31	155	0.4
creamed	1 cup	217	26	126	0.3
American Cheese					
processed	1 ounce	106	6	124	0.1
Milk					
whole	1 cup	150	8	291	0.1
non-fat	1 cup	86	8	302	0.1
Egg	large, raw	77	6	25	0.6
Beef ground					
broiled medium					
(lean with 21%	2.9 ounce				
fat)	patty	223	15	9	1.7
Watermelon					
Chunks	1 cup	51	1	13	0.3

Food	Amount				
Bread Whole wheat	1 slice	61	2	18	0.9
Oatmeal, cooked	1 cup	150	7	22	1.6
Lentils, cooked	1 cup	230	18	37	6.6
Green beans, cooked, drained, frozen cut	1 cup	35	2	62	1.1
Broccoli, frozen, boiled	1 cup	50	5	100	1.1
Cabbage, raw, finely shredded	1 cup	16	1	32	0.4
Collards, frozen boiled	1 cup	62	5	357	1.9
Kale, frozen, boiled	1 cup	40	4	180	1.2
RDA female 25-50 non-pregnant, non-lactating		2200	50	1000	15
RDA male 25-50		2900	63	1000	10

Spices For Vegetarian Cookery

Types and amounts of spices will vary according to your cooking style. Below are some combinations that have proved to work well. Experiment and enjoy!

ALLSPICE

cakes
breads
baked fruit
beverages

CELERY SEED

soups
coleslaw
potato salad
casseroles
mayonnaise

CHILI POWDER

stews
bean dishes

CINNAMON

oatmeal
breads
teas
apple dishes
cottage cheese
fruit dishes

CUMIN

Mexican dishes
spreads
chili

CURRY POWDER

Indian dishes
rice dishes
tofu
salads

GARLIC POWDER

Italian dishes
beans
salads
vegetables
soups
dips and spreads

MARJORAM

stews
squash
soups

MINT

vegetables
frozen desserts
tea
tabbouli

NUTMEG

apple pie
cheese dishes
desserts

OREGANO

beans
pizza
Mexican dishes
tomato dishes
vegetables
Italian dishes
chili

PAPRIKA

hash browns
vegetables
salads
rice
casseroles
cottage cheese

PARSLEY

salads
bread stuffing
dips
soups
stews

ROSEMARY

dips and spreads
vegetables
soups

TARRAGON

green salads
tomato dishes

THYME

peas and carrots
cheese dishes
onion soup

Nutritional Information

SOURCES OF PROTEIN
Chickpeas, lentils, and other dried beans and peas; nuts and seeds; and many common foods such as potatoes, pasta, greens, and bread quickly add to your protein intake.

SOURCES OF IRON
Tofu and other soy products, lentils, split peas, chick peas, collards, potatoes, dried fruit, and watermelon.

SOURCES OF VITAMIN B-12
Fortified breakfast cereals such as Grape-Nuts, some brands of nutritional yeast such as Red Star's Vegetarian Support Formula, some meat analogs, and some fortified soy milk. Read labels.

SOURCES OF CALCIUM
Calcium-fortified orange juice or soy milk, kale, collards, broccoli, tofu, dried figs, dried beans.

VEGETARIAN FOODS HIGH IN FAT
Cheeses, butter, avocado, oil, nuts, whole milk, coconut, margarine, and eggs. Vegetables and fruits contain negligible cholesterol; however, some contain saturated fat.

EGG REPLACER TIPS
1 small banana for 1 egg
2 Tablespoons arrowroot starch or cornstarch for 1 egg

True or False?

1. Vegetarians have to worry about combining proteins.

2. Milk is the only good source of calcium.

3. Vegetarians have to worry about vitamin B12.

4. To be a vegetarian, I have to shop in a health food store and spend a lot of money on groceries.

5. Vegetarian cooking is complicated. I have to change my whole lifestyle to be a vegetarian.

6. Becoming a vegetarian will help me lose weight.

7. Animals in most food advertisements are smiling because they enjoy the good treatment given on farms.

ANSWERS:

1. **FALSE** Vegetarians easily meet their protein needs by eating a varied diet, as long as they consume enough calories to maintain their weight. It is not necessary to plan combinations of foods. A mixture of proteins throughout the day will provide enough essential amino acids. (See "Position of The American Dietetic Association: Vegetarian Diets," JADA, November 1997, and A Vegetarian Sourcebook by Keith Akers).

In using the concept of limiting amino acids, many people wrongly assumed this meant there was none of that amino acid in the food. In fact, most foods contain at least some of all essential amino acids. Exceptions are some fruits and empty calorie or junk foods.

Another important fact is that the body maintains a relatively constant supply of essential amino acids in what is called the amino acid pool. This pool is made up of amino acids from endogenous sources (digestive secretions and desquamated cells) with only a small portion from the diet. The ability of the body to recycle amino acids reassures us that essential amino acids do not need to be eaten in any specific pattern of mealtime or type of food.

Again, the points to remember are to consume a variety of wholesome foods including some protein-rich vegetables and obtain sufficient calories.

2. **FALSE** One cup of whole milk has about 291 mg. of calcium. One cup of cooked collard greens has 357 mg. of calcium. One hundred grams of whole milk has about 118 mg. while one hundred grams of tofu (72 calories) has about 128 mg. of calcium.

3. **FALSE** Most vegetarians eat eggs or dairy products which contain B-12. Vegetarians generally are able to meet their B-12 needs from these sources. Supplements are not necessary. If you do not consume eggs or milk, B-12 can easily be obtained from fortified foods such as Red Star's Vegetarian Support Formula brand of nutritional yeast, Grape-Nuts cereal, and some soy analogs. Many other common foods also have B-12. As in any diet, it is helpful to read labels.

4. **FALSE** You can continue to shop at your local supermarket. If you stay away from processed foods and expensive cheeses, a vegetarian diet will probably be much cheaper than a meat-based diet. Compare the price of a salad bar to a steak dinner!

5. **FALSE** Like every other diet, vegetarianism can be complicated or simple. If you are eating eggs and milk, there are no special considerations for a vegetarian diet. You can continue to eat in the same restaurants and order foods such as eggplant subs, spaghetti, salad bars, French fries, and so on. An added bonus is that you probably will save money by ordering these types of dishes. Vegans need to make sure they consume a reliable source of vitamin B-12.

6. **FALSE** Again, a vegetarian diet is like any other diet. Fat has twice as many calories as carbohydrates and proteins. If you have a normal metabolism, and over consume high-fat foods such as high-fat dairy products, peanut butter, avocados, or cook with too much oil, and do not burn up or eliminate these excess calories, you will probably gain weight no matter what the sources of these calories.

7. **FALSE** In our observations of animals before slaughter, we have not seen any smiling animals. In order to raise animals for food economically, the animals are kept in crowded conditions. Cows are penned up for several months before slaughter without being allowed to exercise. This prevents the meat from becoming tough. One chicken house could easily contain thousands of chickens, who have very short lives, and do not get to see outside sunlight. Factory farm animals are usually fed antibiotics to prevent illnesses.

Suggested Resources

Akers, Keith. A Vegetarian Sourcebook, Vegetarian Press, 1993.

Gandhi, Mahatma. Gandhi, An Autobiography, Beacon Press 1971.

Melina, Vesanto, et. al. Becoming Vegetarian, Book Publishing Company, 1995.

Messina, Virginia, and Mark Messina. The Vegetarian Way. Crown Publishing Group, 1996.

"Position of The American Dietetic Association: Vegetarian Diets," Journal of The American Dietetic Association, Vol. 97:11, 1997.

Robertson, Laurel, et. al. The New Laurel's Kitchen, Ten Speed Press, 1986.

Seventh-day Adventist Dietetic Association The Diet Manual, 1989. Includes vegetarian meal plans used by dietitians in hospitals.

Singer, Peter. Animal Liberation, Avon Books, 1975.

United States Department of Agriculture, Nutritive Value of Foods, 1981.

Beauty Without Cruelty, 175 W. 12th St., New York, NY 10011. Lists alternatives to animal products.

Center for Science in the Public Interest, 1875 Connecticut Ave. NW, Washington, DC 20009. Write for their publications lists. They publish a newsletter, books, and full color posters.

Jewish Vegetarians of North America, 6938 Reliance Rd., Federalsburg, MD 21632; (410) 754-5550.

People for the Ethical Treatment of Animals (PETA), 501 Front St., Norfolk, VA 23510; (757) 622-7382. They promote activism and animal rights.

Physicians Committee for Responsible Medicine, PO Box 6322, Washington, DC 20015.

The Vegetarian Resource Group, PO Box 1463, Baltimore, MD 21203; (410) 366-8343; web site: www.vrg.org

Index

Vegetarian Resource Group Information

Publications by The Vegetarian Resource Group include: *Meatless Meals for Working People—Quick and Easy Vegetarian Recipes* $12; *Simply Vegan—Quick Vegetarian Meals* $13; *Conveniently Vegan—Turn Packaged Foods into Delicious Vegetarian Dishes* $15; *Vegan Handbook—Over 200 Delicious Recipes, Meal Plans, and Vegetarian Resources for All Ages* $20; *The Lowfat Jewish Vegetarian Cookbook—Healthy Traditions from Around the World* $15; *No Cholesterol Passover Recipes* $10; and *Vegetarian Journal's Guide to Natural Foods Restaurants in the U.S. and Canada* $16. To join The Vegetarian Resource Group, order books, ask questions, or find out about local vegetarian groups in your area, write or send payment to The Vegetarian Resource Group, PO Box 1463, Baltimore, MD 21203. You can also call (410) 366-8343 to charge your order or e-mail us at <vrg@vrg.org>.

Join The Vegetarian Resource Group and receive the bi-monthly 36-page *Vegetarian Journal*. This non-profit educational organization works on a local and national level to educate others about vegetarianism. Membership is $20 per year in the U.S.; $30 in Mexico and Canada; and $42 for other foreign countries.

Membership Application

Name _____

Address _____

_____ Zip Code _____

Telephone Number _____

Send payment to The Vegetarian Resource Group, PO Box 1463, Baltimore, MD 21203 or charge your membership over the phone by calling (410) 366-8343. Additionally, you can join VRG or purchase books on our website at <**www.vrg.org**>.